Arthur Henry Bullen

More Lyrics from the Song-Books of the Elizabethan Age

Arthur Henry Bullen

More Lyrics from the Song-Books of the Elizabethan Age

ISBN/EAN: 9783744794831

Printed in Europe, USA, Canada, Australia, Japan

Cover: Foto ©Thomas Meinert / pixelio.de

More available books at **www.hansebooks.com**

MORE LYRICS

FROM THE SONG-BOOKS OF THE ELIZABETHAN AGE:

EDITED BY

A H BULLEN.

LONDON:
JOHN C. NIMMO,
14, KING WILLIAM STREET, STRAND, W.C.
1888.

CHISWICK PRESS:—C. WHITTINGHAM AND CO., TOOKS COURT,
CHANCERY LANE.

PREFACE.

SOME months ago I issued a collection of "Lyrics from the Song-books of the Elizabethan Age," which was intended to serve as a companion volume to the Poetical Miscellanies published in England at the close of the sixteenth and the beginning of the seventeenth centuries. As many of the choicest poems in that collection were unknown even to specialists, I was confident that the value of my anthology would be recognized; and my expectations were not deceived. While the book was passing through the press I had already begun to go over the ground again, and I soon found that materials for a second collection—equal in interest to the first—were growing upon my hands. The present volume is not large, but it represents no inconsiderable amount of labour and research, for I have made it my aim to include only such poems as are, in Izaak Walton's phrase, "choicely good." I shall not reprint the two volumes of my anthology in their present form; but, pursuing my refining process, I shall discard about one-third of the contents of the two series, and shall publish the remaining two-thirds in a single volume for the use of that wider public to which I have not hitherto appealed.

In the preface to the former collection I endeavoured to bring to notice the claims of a true poet, who has been too long neglected—Thomas Campion. It gives me pleasure to know that my efforts have been successful; and I am convinced that no future historians of English poetry will venture, as their predecessors have done, to ignore a lyrist who is worthy to rank with Shelley and Burns. I have read Campion's song-books many times, always with increased delight. He holds among Elizabethan song-writers the place that is held by Meleager in the Greek Anthology: for tenderness and for depth of feeling, for happiness of phrase and for chaste artistic perfection, he is supreme. One of his contemporaries, John Davies of Hereford, who was himself a genuine poet, though he wrote far too much and seldom did himself justice, addressed to Campion a sonnet which contains words of neat and appropriate praise:—

> "Never did lyrics' more than happy strains,
> Strained out of Art by Nature so with ease,
> So purely hit the moods and various veins
> Of music and her hearers as do these.
> So thou canst cure the body and the mind,
> Rare doctor, with thy two-fold soundest art:

> Hippocrates hath taught thee the one kind,
> Apollo and the Muse the other part:
> And both so well that thou with both dost please,
> The mind with pleasure and the corps with ease."

"Strained out of Art by Nature so with ease!" Davies has here just hit the mark. As we read Campion's lyrics we feel that the poet could without effort beat out of our rough English speech whatever music he chose. Whether he is pensively contemplating the flight of Time (p. 19), or treads the downs with the Fairy-queen Proserpina (p. 42), or sings an epithalamium that Catullus might have envied (p. 78), or falls prostrate at the throne of grace (p. 126),—to every varying mood the lyre-strings are responsive. Never a false or jarring note; no cheap tricks and mannerisms; everywhere ease and simplicity. From Campion's song-books[1] I

---

[1] In the former collection I tentatively assigned the publication of Campion's "Third and Fourth Books of Airs" to the year 1613. Mr. Barclay Squire, of the British Museum, who has given me much friendly aid in my researches, points out to me that the date of publication could not have been earlier than 1617. The "Third Book" is dedicated to Sir Thomas Mounson (or Monson), and in the dedicatory address Campion writes:—

> "Since now those clouds, that lately overcast
> Your fame and fortune, are dispersed at last;
> And now since all to you fair greetings make,
> Some out of love and some for pity's sake;
> Shall I but with a common style salute
> Your new enlargement, or stand only mute?

have again drawn freely, and I have also selected some lyrics from his masques. It has sometimes occurred to me that William Drummond of Hawthornden misquoted the remark made by Ben Jonson on the subject of masque-writing. Jonson is reported by Drummond to have said that "next himself only Fletcher and Chapman could make a masque." As Chapman had little ability in that direction, it is far from improbable that Jonson named not Chapman, but Campion. The two names, spoken in conversation, are not very dissimilar in sound, and Drummond may easily have fallen into error. But be this as it may (and I merely throw out the suggestion at a venture), nobody who has read Campion's masques can fail to be struck by their elegance and beauty.

Now a few words as to the unique books and MSS. quoted in the present volume. To Mr. Halliwell-Phillipps I am deeply indebted for permission to

> I, to whose trust and care you durst commit
> Your pined health when art despaired of it?"

Mounson was examined in 1615 with reference to the Overbury trial; the warrant for his arrest was issued in October, 1615; he was liberated on bail in October, 1616; and his pardon was granted in February, 1616-17 ("Cal. State Papers, Dom. 1611-18"). His son, John Mounson, to whom the "Fourth Book of Airs" is dedicated, was born in 1599. From Chamberlain's letters to Carlton it appears that in 1618 the youth was endeavouring, without much success, to ingratiate himself with King James.

include some charming songs from the unique copy of Morley's "First Book of Airs," 1600, preserved at Hollingbury Copse on the Sussex Downs. If, instead of devoting painful years to the acquisition of Shakespearean rarities, Mr. Halliwell-Phillipps had started in pursuit of the philosopher's stone, I am convinced that he would now be in possession of the precious secret. Who at this time of day would dream of finding the autograph of Shakespeare's schoolmaster, Walter Roche? or of John Combe, to whom Shakespeare left his sword as a mark of respect? Yet here they are at Hollingbury Copse; and here too are the title-deeds of New Place,—the very parchment that Shakespeare held in his hand. Here are a hundred rarities, each of them as difficult to discover as the North-west passage. And here is Morley's unique "First Book of Airs" (not quite perfect unfortunately), which contains the original music of "It was a lover and his lass."

Another unique song-book, which has supplied me with some choice lyrics, is Martin Peerson's "Private Music," 1620. It belongs to the Douce collection in the Bodleian Library. From this book I have taken the sweet and tender lullaby "Upon my lap my sovereign sits;" the graceful and playful dialogue—"Open the door! Who's there within?"—between an eager wooer and a discreet maid; the lover's lament for his mistress' fickleness (p. 15), and other dainty little songs.

There is one song-book which I have sought early and late without success—Robert Jones' "The Muses' Garden of Delights," 1610. In 1812 a copy was in the library of the Marquis of Stafford; and in that year Beloe printed six songs from it in the sixth volume of his "Anecdotes." These six songs I have included in the present collection; and they are so delightful that I am consumed with a desire to see the rest of the contents of the song-book. Marble-hearted must have been the maid who could turn a deaf ear to the appeal beginning:—

> "How many new years have grown old
> Since first your servant old was new !
> How many long hours have I told
> Since first my love was vowed to you !
> And yet, alas ! she doth not know
> Whether her servant love or no."

Surely this is the very perfection of song-writing. No less perfect, in a sprightlier vein, is the sobered lover's humorous description of the life he had led under love's thraldom:—

> "Once did my thoughts both ebb and flow,
>   As passion did them move;
> Once did I hope, straight fear again,—
>   And then I was in love;"

or the ironical farewell to Cupid:—

> "Soft, Cupid, soft, there is no haste,
> For all unkindness gone and past;
> Since thou wilt needs forsake me so,
> Let us part friends before thou go."

A special favourite of mine (which I must quote entire) is the warning to heedless youth:—

> "The sea hath many thousand sands,
> The sun hath motes as many;
> The sky is full of stars, and love
> As full of woes as any:
> Believe me, that do know the elf,
> And make no trial by thyself.
>
> It is in truth a pretty toy
> For babes to play withal;
> But O the honies of our youth
> Are oft our age's gall!
> Self-proof in time will make thee know
> He was a prophet told thee so:
>
> A prophet that, Cassandra-like,
> Tells truth without belief;
> For headstrong youth will run his race
> Although his goal be grief:
> Love's martyr, when his heat is past,
> Proves Care's confessor at the last."

I trust that I may yet be able to trace the missing volume, but hitherto my inquiries have been fruitless. The Royal College of Music possesses one unique book of Robert Jones—his "Ultimum Vale," 1608—from which I quoted in my former collection, and which I have again consulted for the present series; but many of the choicest poems in that song-book were printed in Davison's "Poetical Rhapsody."

From early MS. music-books I have also drawn freely. Of these there is a large and important collection in the library of Christ Church, Oxford; and I desire to thank the college authorities[1] for their kindness in allowing me to make selections from their treasures. It is of course difficult in dealing with MS. poetry to determine whether any particular poem is already in print or is absolutely new. The quantity of printed verse of the early seventeenth century is so large that one can seldom pronounce with certainty that such and such poems are inaccessible. I have examined many scores of volumes of Elizabethan and Jacobean poems, and my experience has shown me that nine-tenths of the contents of these MS. collections are extant in printed copies. Hereafter I intend to publish the results of my explorations in this attractive field of research, though I dare not venture to hope that my labours will be crowned with very brilliant success. But to return to the Christ Church MSS. I have chosen from that collection fourteen songs. All of them (so far as my present knowledge goes)—with the exception of "Are women fair and are they sweet?" which is a variation of a poem found in Davison's "Poetical

---

[1] I have particularly to thank the courteous librarian, Rev. T. Vere Bayne.

Rhapsody "—are published for the first time. The noble verses beginning "Yet if his majesty our sovereign lord," cannot fail to attract the reader's attention. I doubt whether it would be possible for me to have lost memory of that poem if I had ever seen it in print. Verse so stately, so simple, so flawless, is not lightly forgotten. The detailed description of the preparations made by a loyal subject for the coming of his "earthly king" is marvellously impressive. Few could have dealt with common household objects—tables and chairs and candles and the rest—in so dignified a spirit. Our poet has triumphed over the difficulties :—

> "'Set me fine Spanish tables in the hall,
> See they be fitted all;
> Let there be room to eat,
> And order taken that there want no meat.
> See every sconce and candlestick made bright,
> That without tapers they may give a light.
> Look to the presence: are the carpets spread,
> The dais o'er the head,
> The cushions in the chairs,
> And all the candles lighted on the stairs?
> Perfume the chamber, and in any case
> Let each man give attendance in his place.'"

It would be hard to improve on that description. Then the contrast between these preparations made for an earthly king and the reception provided for the King of Heaven !—

> "But at the coming of the King of Heaven
> All's set at six and seven :

> We wallow in our sin,
> Christ cannot find a chamber in the inn.
> We entertain him always like a stranger,
> And as at first still lodge him in the manger."

The volume which contains this fine poem has more than one lyric, set to music, of Henry Vaughan the Silurist. Am I right in surmising that this unpublished poem is also by Vaughan? I know no other devotional poet who could have written it. But, whether it be Vaughan's or not, I am glad to include it in my anthology. I trust that the other Christ Church songs will also be acceptable. The odd little snatch "Hey nonny no!/ Men are fools that wish to die!" almost takes one's breath away by the vehemence of its rapture. "Daphnis came on a summer's day" is as good as the best things in Bateson's madrigals (no slight praise), and "Are you that she than whom no fairer is?" might have come from one of Robert Jones' song-books. The frog's wooing of the crab ("There was a frog swum in the lake") is a capital piece of fooling, almost worthy to rank with Ravenscroft's "It was the frog in the well." It was set to music by Alfonso Ferrabosco, but is not found in that composer's printed "Airs." The song "Where would coy Aminta run?" seems to be familiar, but I have not yet been able to trace it. Of James Hart, who composed the music, I can find no particulars.

From my examination of the Christ Church MSS. I have been able, besides giving new matter, to record variations in the text of printed songs. Thus, in Bateson's "If I seek to enjoy the fruits of my pain," I have not only improved the text of the printed copy by reference to the MS. copy, but I have restored three verses which Bateson had entirely omitted. More important are the variations in Campion's "I must complain, yet do enjoy my love," where the second and third stanzas of the MS. copy (see p. 155) differ entirely from the printed text.

I had hoped to discover some choice new songs among the MSS. in the Music School at Oxford, but I found that almost everything of interest was accessible in printed collections. Still I contrived to glean a few snatches. My researches among the MS. music-books in the British Museum were hardly more successful. The dialogue between Endymion and Phœbe—"Lovely shepherd, ope thine eye"—was indeed well worth rescuing from obscurity. If it has been printed before, I must apologize to the more learned reader for my ignorance. The pretty cradle-song, "My little sweet darling, my comfort and joy," set to music by William Byrd, is not found in any of the composer's printed song-books; nor do I remember to have met "Phillis, a herd-maid dainty," which reads like a translation of an Italian madrigal.

It will be seen that I have selected half-a-dozen songs from Dr. John Wilson's "Cheerful Airs," published at Oxford in 1660. Those who are not acquainted with Wilson's "Airs" may think that I have stepped out of my proper period in quoting from a book of that late date; but I assure them that the poetry belongs almost entirely to Elizabethan or Jacobean times. The same remark applies to John Forbes' "Cantus," first published at Aberdeen in 1661, which is largely composed of songs from the collections of Campion, Dowland, Jones, and others. From Forbes I have taken only one poem ("Joy to the person of my love"), the text of which I have corrected from a MS. copy preserved in the Advocates' Library at Edinburgh.

In the former series I gave copious extracts from Dowland's song-books; and I have quoted largely from them in the present volume. William Corkine and Francis Pilkington are again among the leading contributors; nor have I neglected John Attey and Alfonso Ferrabosco (the friend of Ben Jonson and composer of the music to "Come, my Celia"). From John Danyel's "Songs," 1606, I have chosen the singularly fine devotional poem "If I could shut the gate against my thoughts," the address to "Time, cruel Time," and some verse of lighter quality. William Byrd is again represented, chiefly in his meditative mood. One sonnet ("Those eyes that set my fancy on a fire") is taken from that very rare book—preserved under glass in a show-case at the British Museum—William Barley's "New Book of Tabliture," 1596. The conclusion of this sonnet is in the great Elizabethan style:—

> "O eyes that pierce our hearts without remorse!
> O hairs of right that wear a royal crown!
> O hands that conquer more than Cæsar's force!
> O wit that turns huge kingdoms upside down!"

Many volumes of selected sonnets have been published in recent years; but you may search them all without finding this sonnet from Barley's "New Book of Tabliture."

I need not describe at greater length the contents of the present volume; but I wish to say a few words in regard to the plan on which my anthology has been put together. The reader must clearly understand that the present collection and its predecessor do not for a moment claim to be a representative anthology of the whole wealth of Elizabethan lyrical poetry. I have conducted the reader through only one tract of those wonderful Realms of Gold. I have avoided well-beaten highways and have preferred to guide him by lonely paths through shy coverts. It is solely with the old song-books, the music-books, that I have dealt. Some of these are extant only in unique exemplars preserved in the library of the British Museum, the Bodleian, the library of the

Royal College of Music,[1] or in private libraries: for others I have had to go to MSS. in the British Museum and at Oxford. I can say with a clear conscience that, in order to make my anthology as interesting as possible, I have shirked no labour, and that I have tried to keep the standard of excellence in all cases high. Well-known poems, or poems that ought to be well known, I have avoided. For instance I have not included such a poem as "His golden locks Time hath to silver turn'd," which is set to music in Dowland's "First Book;" for it was written by George Peele (perhaps the best thing he wrote) and is familiar to the generality of readers. Again, I have omitted "Shall I tell you whom I love?" which is found in John Attey's "Airs," 1622; for the author was William Browne, and I take it for granted that "Britannia's Pastorals" is a well-thumbed classic. Yet I must own that I have not been quite consistent; for the reader will find a sonnet (set to music by Martin Peerson) taken from Sidney's "Arcadia," and a short poem (from Dowland's "First Book") that was printed in 1630 among the "Works" of Fulke Greville, Lord Brooke. A few of the poems in the present volume are also to be found in Davison's "Poetical Rhapsody."

[1] I should be ungrateful if I neglected to acknowledge the courtesy that I received from Sir George Grove, the distinguished director of that excellent institution.

Eloquar an sileam? Song-writing is now almost as completely a lost art as play-writing. Our poets, who ought to make "music and sweet poetry agree," leave the writing of songs to meaner hands. Contrast the poor thin wretched stuff that one hears to-day in drawing-rooms with the rich full-throated songs of Campion and Dowland. O what a fall is there, my countrymen! In Elizabethan times music was "married to immortal verse." Let us hope that the present separation will not always continue.

INDEX OF FIRST LINES.

INDEX OF FIRST LINES.

	PAGE
A FEIGNED friend by proof I find (William Byrd)	1
A stranger here, as all my fathers were (John Amner)	2
Ah me! my wonted joys forsake me (Thomas Weelkes)	2
Ah sweet, alas! when first I saw those eyes (George Kirbye)	2
Ambitious love hath forced me to aspire (William Byrd)	3
And is it night? are they thine eyes that shine (Robert Jones)	3
And think ye, nymphs, to scorn at Love (William Byrd)	4
Are women fair and are they sweet (Christ Church MS.)	4
Are you what your fair looks express (Thomas Campion)	5
Art thou that she than whom no fairer is (Christ Church MS.)	6
At her fair hands how have I grace entreated (Robert Jones)	7
Awake, sweet love! thou art returned (John Dowland)	9
Awake, thou spring of speaking grace! mute rest becomes not thee (Thomas Campion)	10
Ay me, she frowns; my mistress is offended (Francis Pilkington)	11
Be thou then my Beauty named (Thomas Campion)	12
Beauty is but a painted hell (Thomas Campion)	13
Blame not my cheeks, though pale with love they be (Campion and Rosseter)	13
Blush, my rude present; blushing, yet say this (Thomas Vautor)	14
Buzz, buzz, buzz (Add. MS.)	14
Camella fair tripped o'er the plain (Thomas Bateson)	15
Can a maid that is well bred (Martin Peerson)	15
Care for thy soul as thing of greatest price (William Byrd)	16
Cease, troubled thoughts, to sigh or sigh yourselves to death (Robert Jones)	17
Change me, O heavens, into the ruby stone (John Wilbye)	18
Come away, armed with love's delights (Thomas Campion)	18
Come, cheerful day, part of my life to me (Thomas Campion)	19
Come, lusty ladies, come, come, come (Christ Church MS.)	20
Come, pretty wag, and sing (Martin Peerson)	20
Come, Sorrow, come, sit down and mourn with me (Thomas Morley)	21

INDEX OF FIRST LINES.

P

Come, ye heavy states of night (*John Dowland*) . . . . .
Content thyself with thy estate (*Richard Carlton*) . . . . .
Cupid, in a bed of roses (*Thomas Bateson*) . . . . .

Daphnis came on a summer's day (*Christ Church MS.*)
Dear, do not your fair beauty wrong (*Musica Antiqua*) . .
Deceitful fancy, why delud'st thou me (*John Coperario*) . . .
Did ever man thus love as I (*Robert Jones*) . . . .
Disdain me still that I may ever love (*John Dowland*) . . .
Disdain, that so doth fill me (*Robert Jones*) . . . .
Do not, O do not prize thy beauty at too high a rate (*Robert Jones*)
Drown not with tears, my dearest Love (*Alfonso Ferrabosco*) . .

Fain I would, but oh I dare not (*Alfonso Ferrabosco*) . . . .
Fain would I my love disclose (*Thomas Campion*) . . . .
Fair Hebe, when dame Flora meets (*Thomas Bateson*) . .
Fair is my love, my dear and only jewel (*Michael Este*) . . .
Fair is the rose, yet fades with heat or cold (*Orlando Gibbons*) . .
Fair women like fair jewels are (*Robert Jones*) . . . .
Farewell, dear love! since thou wilt needs be gone (*Robert Jones*) .
Fie, fie, fie! what a coil is here (*Robert Jones*) . . . . . .
Flow not so fast, ye fountains (*John Dowland*) . . . . .
Follow thy fair sun, unhappy shadow (*Campion and Rosseter*) . .
Fond Love is blind, blind therefore lovers be (*Thomas Bateson*) . .
Fondness of man to love a she (*Dr. John Wilson*) . . . .

Go, nightly cares, the enemy to rest (*John Dowland*) . . .
Greedy lover, pause awhile (*Dr. John Wilson*) . . . .

Harden now thy tired heart with more than flinty rage (*Thomas
    Campion*) . . . .
Hark, all you ladies that do sleep (*Campion and Rosseter*) . . .
Heigh ho (*Pammelia*) . . . .
Her fair inflaming eyes (*Thomas Campion*) . . .
Her hair the net of golden wire (*Thomas Bateson*) .
Hey nonny no (*Christ Church MS.*)
Hold, cruel Love, O hold! I yield (*MS. Mus. Sch.*) . .
How eas'ly wert thou chained (*Thomas Campion*) . . .
How many new years have grown old (*Robert Jones*) . .

I care not for these ladies (*Campion and Rosseter*) . . . .
I heard a noise and wished for a sight (*Thomas Bateson*) . . .
I heard of late that Love was fall'n asleep (*John Bartlet*) . . .
I know not what, yet that I feel is much (*Robert Jones*) . . . .
I must complain, yet do enjoy my love (*Thomas Campion*) . . .

INDEX OF FIRST LINES.

	PAGE
If I could shut the gate against my thoughts (John Danyel)	52
If I seek to enjoy the fruits of my pain (Thomas Bateson)	53
If in thine heart thou nourish ill (William Byrd)	54
If love loves truth then women do not love (Thomas Campion)	54
If she forsake me, I must die (Campion and Rosseter)	55
If when I die, to Hell's eternal shade (MS. Mus. Sch.)	56
If women can be courteous when they list (Richard Carlton)	56
In a grove of trees of myrtle (John Attey)	56
In fields abroad, where trumpets shrill do sound (William Byrd)	57
Is not that my fancy's Queen (Martin Peerson)	58
It fell on a summer's day (Campion and Rosseter)	59
Joy in thy hope, the earnest of thy love (Robert Jones)	60
Joy to the person of my love (John Forbes)	61
Lais, now old, that erst attempting lass (Orlando Gibbons)	63 64
Let dread of pain for sin in after-time (Thomas Greaves)	63
Let not thy blackness move thee to despair (Christ Church MS.)	64
Lie down, poor heart, and die awhile for grief (Robert Jones)	64
Like as the gentle heart itself bewrays (Richard Carlton)	65
Lock up, fair lids, the treasure of my heart (Martin Peerson)	66
Love her no more, herself she doth not love (Martin Peerson)	66
Love, if a God thou art (Robert Jones)	67
Love in thy youth, fair maid; be wise (Walter Porter)	67
Love me or not, love her I must or die (Thomas Campion)	68
Lovely shepherd, ope thine eye (Add. MS.)	68
Mistress mine, well may you fare (Thomas Morley)	70
Mourn, mourn! day is with darkness fled (John Dowland)	71
Music, some think, no music is (Thomas Bateson)	72
My complaining is but feigning (Robert Jones)	72
My little sweet darling, my comfort and joy (Add. MS.)	72
My mistress after service due (Thomas Bateson)	73
My sins are like the hairs upon my head (Christ Church MS.)	73
Nay, let me weep, though others' tears be spent (Orlando Gibbons)	74
Neither buskin now, nor bays (Thomas Campion)	75
Noell, adieu, adieu! thou Court's delight (Thomas Weelkes)	76
Now cease, my wand'ring eyes (John Dowland)	76
Now, Cupid, look about thee (Thomas Robinson)	77
Now hath Flora robbed her bowers (Thomas Campion)	78
Now peep, bo-peep, thrice happy blest mine eyes (Francis Pilkington)	79
O love, where are thy shafts, thy quiver, and thy bow (Thomas Campion)	80

	PAGE
O my poor eyes, the sun whose shine (Robert Jones)	81
O precious time, created by the might (Martin Peerson)	82
O sweet flower, too quickly fading (John Coperario)	82
O what hath overwrought (John Dowland)	83
Of Neptune's empire let us sing (Thomas Campion)	84
On a fair morning, as I came by the way (Thomas Morley)	85
Once did my thoughts both ebb and flow (Robert Jones)	85
One woman scarce of twenty (Thomas Bateson)	86
Open the door! Who's there within (Martin Peerson)	87
Perplexed sore am I (Robert Jones)	88
Phillis, a herd-maid dainty (Add. MS.)	88
Reprove not love, though fondly thou hast lost (Campion and Rosseter)	89
Respect my faith, regard my service past (Thomas Campion)	90
Rest awhile, you cruel cares (John Dowland)	90
Say, fond Love, what seeks thou here (Add. MS.)	91
Say, Love, if ever thou didst find (John Dowland)	92
See where she flies enraged from me (Campion and Rosseter)	93
See where my love a-maying goes (Francis Pilkington)	94
Shall a smile or guileful glance (William Corkine)	94
Shall I be with joys deceived (William Corkine)	95
Since just disdain began to rise (Robert Jones)	95
Sing, merry birds, your cheerful notes (Robert Jones)	96
Sly thief, if so you will believe (Michael Este)	96
So quick, so hot, so mad is thy fond suit (Thomas Campion)	97
So saith my fair and beautiful Lycoris (Musica Transalpina)	98
So sweet is thy discourse to me (Thomas Campion)	98
Soft, Cupid, soft, there is no haste (Robert Jones)	99
Sometime she would and sometime not (Giles Farnaby)	99
Stay, Corydon, thou swain (John Wilbye)	100
Sweet Gemma, when I first beheld thy beauty (Thomas Bateson)	100
Sweet, if you like and love me still (Robert Jones)	101
Sweet, let me go! sweet, let me go (William Corkine)	102
Sweet, those trammels of your hair (Thomas Bateson)	102
Sweet, yet cruel unkind is she (Christ Church MS.)	103
Tell me, O Love, when shall it be (Alfonso Ferrabosco)	103
The cypress curtain of the night is spread (Campion and Rosseter)	104
The eagle's force subdues each bird that flies (William Byrd)	105
The fountains smoke and yet no flames they show (Robert Jones)	105
The Gordian knot, which Alexander great (John Attey)	106
The greedy wretch that surfeits on his gold (Christ Church MS.)	107

INDEX OF FIRST LINES.

	PAGE
The nightingale in silent night (Thomas Bateson)	107
The Queen of Paphos, Erycine (John Bartlet)	107
The sea hath many thousand sands (Robert Jones)	108
The spring of joy is dry (Martin Peerson)	109
The witless boy that blind is to behold (Richard Carlton)	110
There is none, O none but you (Thomas Campion)	110
There was a frog swum in the lake (Christ Church MS.)	111
Thine eyes so bright (Robert Jones)	112
Those eyes that set my fancy on a fire (William Barley)	112
Those spots upon my lady's face appearing (Thomas Weelkes)	113
Thou joyest, fond boy, to be by many loved (Thomas Campion)	113
Thou sent'st to me a heart was crowned (MS. Mus. Sch.)	114
Though me you disdain to view (John Hilton)	114
Though you are young and I am old (Campion and Rosseter)	115
Three times a day my prayer is (Thomas Weelkes)	115
Thule, the period of cosmography (Thomas Weelkes)	116
Thyrsis and Milla, arm in arm together (Thomas Morley)	116
Time, cruel Time, canst thou subdue that brow (John Danyel)	117
Time's eldest son, Old Age, the heir of Ease (John Dowland)	118
"To bed, to bed!" she calls and never ceaseth (Michael Este)	119
To-morrow is the marriage-day (Thomas Weelkes)	119
To music bent is my retired mind (Thomas Campion)	120
Trust not too much, fair youth, unto thy feature (Orlando Gibbons)	120
Truth-trying Time shall cause my mistress say (William Corkine)	121
Turn back, you wanton flyer (Campion and Rosseter)	121
Turn in, my Lord, turn into me (Christ Church MS.)	122
Unkind, is this the meed of lovers' pain (Thomas Vautor)	123
Unquiet thoughts, your civil slaughter stint (John Dowland)	123
Upon my lap my sovereign sits (Martin Peerson)	124
Veil, Love, mine eyes! O hide from me (Thomas Campion)	125
Victorious Time, whose winged feet do fly (Christ Church MS.)	125
View me, Lord, a work of Thine (Thomas Campion)	126
Were I made juror of that quest (Add. MS.)	127
What delight can they enjoy (John Danyel)	128
What if I seek for love of thee (Robert Jones)	128
What is it all that men possess, among themselves conversing (Thomas Campion)	129
What saith my dainty darling (Thomas Morley)	130
What would any man desire (Dr. John Wilson)	131
When from my love I look'd for love and kind affection's due (John Bartlet)	132
When I behold my mistress' face (Dr. John Wilson)	132

INDEX OF FIRST LINES.

	PAGE
When I sit reading all alone that secret book (*Robert Jones*)	133
When I was born Lucina cross-legged sate (*William Corkine*)	134
When love on time and measure makes his ground (*Robert Jones*)	134
When on mine eyes her eyes first shone (*Dr. John Wilson*)	135
When on my dear I do demand the due (*Michael Este*)	135
When the god of merry love (*Campion and Rosseter*)	136
When to her lute Corinna sings (*Campion and Rosseter*)	136
When will the fountain of my tears be dry (*Robert Jones*)	137
Where Fancy fond for Pleasure pleads (*William Byrd*)	138
Where lingering fear doth once possess the heart (*Robert Jones*)	139
Where would coy Aminta run (*Christ Church MS.*)	140
Who vows devotion to fair beauty's shrine (*Richard Carlton*)	141
Whoever thinks or hopes of love for love (*John Dowland*)	141
Why canst thou not, as others do (*John Danyel*)	142
Will ye love me, lady sweet (*Thomas Ravenscroft*)	143
Women, what are they? Changing weathercocks (*Robert Jones*)	143
Wounded I am, and dare not seek relief (*William Byrd*)	144
Yet if his majesty our sovereign lord (*Christ Church MS.*)	145
You gentle nymphs that on these meadows play (*Francis Pilkington*)	146
You say you love me, nay, can swear it too (*Dr. John Wilson*)	146
You that pine in long desire (*Francis Pilkington*)	147
Young and simple though I am (*Thomas Campion*)	148
Young Cupid hath proclaimed a bloody war (*Thomas Weelkes*)	149
Your fair looks urge my desire (*Thomas Campion*)	149

MORE LYRICS FROM ELIZABETHAN SONG-BOOKS.

*Let well-tuned words amaze
With harmony divine.*
CAMPION.

MORE LYRICS FROM THE SONG-BOOKS OF THE ELIZABETHAN AGE.

From WILLIAM BYRD'S *Psalms,
Songs, and Sonnets*, 1611.

A FEIGNED friend by proof I find
    To be a greater foe
Than he that with a spiteful mind
    Doth seek my overthrow;
For of the one I can beware,
With craft the other breeds my care.

Such men are like the hidden rocks
    Which in the seas doth lie,
Against the which each ship that knocks
    Is drowned suddenly:
No greater fraud nor more unjust
Than false deceit hid under trust.

From JOHN AMNER'S *Sacred Hymns*, 1615.

A STRANGER here, as all my fathers were
    That went before, I wander to and fro ;
From earth to heaven is my pilgrimage,
  A tedious way for flesh and blood to go :
O Thou that art the way, pity the blind
And teach me how I may Thy dwelling find.

From THOMAS WEELKES' *Madrigals*, 1597.

AH me ! my wonted joys forsake me,
    And deep despair doth overtake me ;
I whilome sung, but now I weep :
Thus sorrows run, when joys do creep.
I wish to live, and yet I die ;
For love hath wrought my misery.

From GEORGE KIRBYE'S *First Set of English Madrigals*, 1597.

AH sweet, alas ! when first I saw those eyes,
    Those eyes so rich with crystal majesty,
Their wounding beauty gan[1] to tyrannise
  And made mine eyes bleed tears full plenteously :
I felt the wound, yet feared I not the deed,
Till ah ! I found my tears did inward bleed.

[1] Old ed., " gan (*then*) to tyrannyze."

From WILLIAM BYRD'S *Psalms,
Sonnets, and Songs,* 1588.

AMBITIOUS love hath forced me to aspire
    The beauties rare which do adorn thy face;
Thy modest life yet bridles my desire,
Whose severe law doth promise me no grace.
But what! may Love live under any law?
No, no, his power exceedeth man's conceit,
Of which the Gods themselves do stand in awe,
For on his frown a thousand torments wait.
Proceed then in this desperate enterprise
With good advice, and follow Love thy guide,
That leads thee to thy wished paradise.
Thy climbing thoughts this comfort take withal:
That, if it be thy foul disgrace to slide,
Thy brave attempt shall yet excuse thy fall.

From ROBERT JONES' *Musical
Dream,* 1609.

AND is it night? are they thine eyes that shine?
    Are we alone, and here? and here, alone?
May I come near, may I but touch thy shrine?
    Is jealousy asleep, and is he gone?
O Gods, no more! silence my lips with thine!
Lips, kisses, joys, hap, blessing most divine!

O come, my dear ! our griefs are turn'd to night,
   And night to joys ; night blinds pale envy's eyes ;
Silence and sleep prepare us our delight,
   O cease we then our woes, our griefs, our cries :
O vanish words ! words do but passions move :
O dearest life ! joy's sweet ! O sweetest love !

From WILLIAM BYRD'S *Songs of
Sundry Natures*, 1589.

AND think ye, nymphs, to scorn at Love,
   As if his fire were but of straws ?
He made the mighty gods above
   To stoop and bow unto his laws ;
And with his shaft of beauty bright
He slays the hearts that scorn his might.—

Love is a fit of pleasure
   Bred out of idle brains ;
His fancies have no measure,
   No more than have his pains :
His vain affections like the weather,
Precise or fond, we wot not whether.

From *Christ Church MS*. K. 3.
43-5. (Music by THOMAS
FORD.)

(1) ARE women fair and are they sweet ?
(2) Most fair and sweet to all that inly love them.
(1) Chaste and discreet ?

(2) Chaste and discreet to all save those that prove them.
(1) Are women wise, are women witty?
(2) Not wise, but they be witty;
Yea, the more the pity.
They are so witty, and in wit so wily,
That be you ne'er so wise they will beguile ye.[1]
(1) Are women saints, are women good?
(2) No saints, nor yet no devils;
Not good, but needful evils.
So angel-like that devils you may not doubt them;
So needful ills that few can live without them.
(1) Are women proud, are women kind?
(2) Yea passing proud, and praise them;
Yea wondrous kind, and please them:
Or so imperious no man may endure them,
Or so kind-hearted any may procure them.

From THOMAS CAMPION'S *Fourth Book of Airs* (circ. 1617).

ARE you what your fair looks express?
    O then be kind!
From law of nature they digress
    Whose form suits not their mind:
Fairness seen in th' outward shape
Is but th' inward beauty's ape.

[1] MS. "you."

Eyes that of earth are mortal made,
    What can they view?
All's but a colour or a shade,
    And neither always true:
Reason's sight, that is etern,
E'en the substance can discern.

Soul is the Man: for who will so
    The body name?
And to that power all grace we owe,
    That decks our living frame.
What or how had housen bin
But for them that dwell therein?

Love in the bosom is begot,
    Not in the eyes;
No beauty makes the eye more hot,
    Her flames the sprite surprise:
Let our loving minds then meet,
For pure meetings are most sweet.

From Christ Church MS, 1. 5. 49.

"ART thou that she than whom no fairer is,
Art thou that she desire so strives to kiss?"
"Say I am: how then?
    Maids may not kiss
    Such wanton-humour'd men."

"Art thou that she the world commends for wit?
Art thou so wise and makest no use of it?"
"Say I am : how then?
My wit doth teach me shun
Such foolish foolish men."

From ROBERT JONES' *Ultimum Vale*, 1608.

AT her fair hands how have I grace entreated
With prayers oft repeated,
Yet still my love is thwarted!
Heart, let her go, for she'll not be converted.
Say, shall she go?
O, no, no, no, no, no!
She is most fair, though she be marble-hearted.

How often have my sighs declared my anguish
Wherein I daily languish,
Yet still she doth procure it!
Heart, let her go, for I cannot endure it.
Say, shall she go?
O, no, no, no, no, no!
She gave the wound, and she alone must cure it.

The trickling tears that down my cheeks have flowed
My love hath often showed,
Yet still unkind I prove her.
Heart, let her go, for nought I do can move her.
Say, shall she go?
O, no, no, no, no, no!
Though me she hate I cannot chuse but love her.

But shall I still a true affection owe[1] her,
    Which prayers, sighs, tears do show her,
    And shall she still disdain me?
Heart, let her go, if they no grace can gain me.
    Say, shall she go?
    O, no, no, no, no, no!
She made me hers and hers she will retain me.

But if the love that hath and still doth burn me
    No love at length return me,
    Out of my thoughts I'll set her:
Heart, let her go, O heart, I pray thee, let her.
    Say, shall she go?
    O, no, no, no, no, no!
Fixed in the heart, how can the heart forget her?

But if I weep and sigh and often wail me
    Till tears, sighs, prayers fail me,
    Shall yet my love persever?[2]
Heart, let her go, if she will right thee never.
    Say, shall she go?
    O no, no, no, no, no!
Tears, sighs, prayers fail, but true love lasteth ever.

[1] This is the reading of the 1608 edition of Davison's *Poetical Rhapsody*. The song-book reads "bear her."
[2] Old form of "persevere."

From JOHN DOWLAND'S *First
Book of Songs or Airs*, 1597.

AWAKE, sweet love! thou art returned!
My heart, which long in absence mourned,
Lives now in perfect joy.
Only herself hath seemed fair,
She only I could love;
She only drave me to despair
When she unkind did prove.

Let love, which never, absent, dies,
Now live for ever in her eyes
Whence came my first annoy!
Despair did make me wish to die
That I my joys might end:
She only, which did make me fly,
My state may now amend.

—If she esteem thee now ought worth,
She will not grieve thy love henceforth,
    Which so despair hath proved.—
Despair hath proved now in me
That love will not unconstant be
    Though long in vain I loved.—

If she at last reward thy love
    And all thy harms repair,
Thy happiness will sweeter prove,
    Raised up from deep despair;
And if that now thou welcome be
    When thou with her doth meet,
She all this while but played with thee
    To make thy joys more sweet.

From Thomas Campion's *Third Book of Airs* (circ. 1617).

AWAKE, thou spring of speaking grace! mute rest becomes not thee :
The fairest women while they sleep, and pictures, equal be.
    O come and dwell in love's discourses !
    Old renewing, new creating.
    The words which thy rich tongue discourses
    Are not of the common rating.

Thy voice is as an Echo clear which music doth beget,
Thy speech is as an oracle which none can counterfeit :
    For thou alone, without offending,
    Hast obtained power of enchanting,
    And I could hear thee without ending,
    Other comfort never wanting.

Some little reason brutish lives with human glory share,
But language is our proper grace from which they severed are.
    As brutes in reason man surpasses,
    Men in speech excel each other :
    If speech be then the best of graces,
    Do it not in slumber smother.

From FRANCIS PILKINGTON'S
First Book of Songs or Airs,
1605.

AY me, she frowns; my mistress is offended;
O pardon, dear, my miss[1] shall be amended.
    My fault from love proceeded,
      It merits grace the rather;
    If I no danger dreaded,
      It was to win your favour.
    Then clear those clouds, then smile on me,
      And let us be good friends:
    Come walk, come talk, come kiss, come see
      How soon our quarrel ends.

Why lours my love and blots so sweet a beauty?
O be appeased with vows, with faith, and duty.
    Give over to be cruel,
      Sith kindness seems you better;
    You have but changed a jewel,
      And Love is not your debtor.
    Then welcome mirth and banish moan,
      Shew pity on your lover;
    Come play, come sport, the thing that's gone
      No sorrow can recover.

Still are you angry and is there no relenting?
O weigh my woes, be moved with my lamenting.
    Alas, my heart is grieved,
      Mine inward soul doth sorrow;

[1] Fault.

Unless I be relieved
  I die before to-morrow.
The coast is clear'd, her count'nance cheer'd,
  I am again in grace ;
Then farewell fear, then come, my dear,
  Let's dally and embrace !

From THOMAS CAMPION'S *Third
Book of Airs* (circ. 1617).

BE thou then my Beauty named,
    Since thy will is to be mine ;
For by that I am enflamed
    Which on all alike doth shine ;
Others may the light admire,
I only truly feel the fire.

But if lofty titles move thee,
    Challenge then a Sovereign's place ;
Say I honour when I love thee,
    Let me call thy kindness Grace :
State and Love things diverse be,
Yet will we teach them to agree.

Or if this be not sufficing,
    Be thou styled my Goddess then :
I will love thee, sacrificing ;
    In thine honour hymns I'll pen :
To be thine, what canst thou more ?
I'll love thee, serve thee, and adore.

> From THOMAS CAMPION'S *Fourth
> Book of Airs* (circ. 1617).

BEAUTY is but a painted hell :
    Ay me, ay me !
She wounds them that admire it,
She kills them that desire it.
  Give her pride but fuel,
  No fire is more cruel.

Pity from every heart is fled :
    Ay me, ay me !
Since false desire could borrow
Tears of dissembled sorrow,
  Constant vows turn truthless,
  Love cruel, Beauty ruthless.

Sorrow can laugh and Fury sing :
    Ay me, ay me !
My raving griefs discover
I lived too true a lover.
  The first step to madness
  Is excess of sadness.

> From CAMPION and ROSSETER'S
> *Book of Airs*, 1601.

BLAME not my cheeks, though pale with love they be ;
  The kindly heat unto my heart is flown
To cherish it that is dismayed by thee,
  Who art so cruel and unsteadfast grown :
For Nature, called for by distressed hearts,
Neglects and quite forsakes the outward parts.

But they whose cheeks with careless blood are stained
  Nurse not one spark of love within their hearts ;
And, when they woo, they speak with passion feigned,
  For their fat love lies in their outward parts :
But in their breasts, where love his court should hold,
Poor Cupid sits and blows his nails for cold.

From THOMAS VAUTOR'S *Songs of divers Airs and Natures*, 1619.

BLUSH, my rude present ; blushing, yet say this,—
  That he that sent thee meant a better thing :
Best meaners oft of their best purpose miss,
  Best runners sometime fail to hit the ring ;
What wants in show he doth supply in mind :
Tell my sweet mistress, saint of woman-kind.

From *Add. MS.* 17792.

BUZZ, buzz, buzz !
  Ring out your kettle
Of purest metal
To settle, to settle,
Your swarm of bees !
For men new wiving
The way to be thriving
Is hiving, hiving ;
Then no time leese[1]
To hive your bees.

[1] Old form of "lose."

From THOMAS BATESON'S *Second
Set of Madrigals*, 1618.

CAMELLA fair tripped o'er the plain,
    I followed quickly after ;
Have overtaken her I would fain,
    And kissed her when I caught her.
But hope being passed her to obtain,
    " Camella ! " loud I call :
She answered me with great disdain,
    " I will not kiss at all."

From MARTIN PEERSON'S *Private Music*, 1620.

CAN a maid that is well bred,
    Hath a blush so lovely red,
Modest looks, wise, mild, discreet,
And a nature passing sweet,

Break her promise, untrue prove,
On a sudden change her love,
Or be won e'er to neglect
Him to whom she vowed respect ?

Such a maid, alas ! I know :
O that weeds 'mongst corn should grow !
Or a rose should prickles have,
Wounding where she ought to save !

I, that did her parts extol,
Will my lavish tongue control:
Outward parts do blind the eyes,
Gall in golden pills oft lies.

Reason, wake, and sleep no more,
Land upon some safer shore,
Think on her and be afraid
Of a faithless fickle maid.

Of a faithless fickle maid
Thus true love is still betrayed:
Yet it is some ease to sing
That a maid is light of wing.

From WILLIAM BYRD'S *Psalms
Sonnets, and Songs*, 1588.

CARE for thy soul as thing of greatest price,
    Made to the end to taste of power divine,
Devoid of guilt, abhorring sin and vice,
   Apt by God's grace to virtue to incline:
Care for it so that by thy reckless train
It be not brought to taste eternal pain.

Care for thy corpse, but chiefly for soul's sake;
   Cut off excess, sustaining food is best;
To vanquish pride, but comely clothing take;
   Seek after skill, deep ignorance detest:
Care so (I say) the flesh to feed and clothe,
That thou harm not thy soul and body both.

Care for the world, to do thy body right ;
　Rack not thy wit to win by wicked ways ;
Seek not to oppress the weak by wrongful might ;
　To pay thy due do banish all delays :
Care to dispend according to thy store,
And in like sort be mindful of the poor.

Care for thy soul as for thy chiefest stay ;
　Care for thy body for the soul's avail ;
Care for the world for body's help alway ;
　Care yet but so as virtue may prevail :
Care in such sort as thou beware of this—
Care keep thee not from heaven and heavenly bliss !

From ROBERT JONES' *Ultimum Vale*, 1608.

CEASE, troubled thoughts, to sigh or sigh yourselves
　　　　to death,
Or kindle not my grief or cool it with your breath :
　　Let not that spirit which made me live
　　Seek thus untimely to deprive
　　　　Me of my life :
　　　　Unequal strife,
That breath which gave me being
Should hasten me to dying !

Cease, melting tears, to stream, stop your uncessant
　　　course,
Which to my sorrow's child are like a fruitful nurse,

From whence death living comfort draws ;
And I myself appear the cause
    Of all my woe ;
    But 'tis not so,
For she, whose beauty won me,
By falsehood hath undone me.

From JOHN WILBYE'S *Second Set of Madrigals*, 1609.

CHANGE me, O heavens into the ruby stone
    That on my love's fair locks doth hang in gold,
Yet leave me speech to her to make my moan,
    And give me eyes her beauties to behold ;
Or if you will not make my flesh a stone,
Make her hard heart seem flesh that now seems none.

From THOMAS CAMPION'S *Two Books of Airs* (circ. 1613).

COME away, armed with love's delights !
    Thy spriteful glances bring with thee !
When love and longing fights,
    They must the sticklers be.
Come quickly, come ! the promised hour is well-nigh spent,
And pleasure, being too much deferred, loseth her best content.

Is she come? Oh how near is she!
   How far yet from this friendly place !
How many steps from me !
   When shall I her embrace !
These arms I'll spread, which only at her sight shall close,
Attending as the starry flower that the sun's noontide knows.

                        From THOMAS CAMPION'S *Two
                        Books of Airs* (circ. 1613).

COME, cheerful day, part of my life to me ;
   For while thou view'st me with thy fading light,
Part of my life doth still depart with thee,
   And I still onward haste to my last night :
Time's fatal wings do ever forward fly,
So every day we live a day we die.

But, O ye nights, ordained for barren rest,
   How are my days deprived of life in you,
When heavy sleep my soul hath dispossest,
   By feigned death life sweetly to renew !
Part of my life in that, you life deny :
So every day we live a day we die.

From Christ Church MS. 1. 5. 49.

COME, lusty ladies, come, come, come!
  With pensive thoughts you pine.
Come, learn the galliard now of[1] us,
For we be masquers [fine].
We sing, we dance, and we rejoice
With mirth in modesty:
Come, ladies, then and take a part,
And, as we sing, dance ye!
Tarranta ta-ta-ta-ta-tararantina, &c.

From MARTIN PEERSON'S Private Music, 1620.

COME, pretty wag, and sing;
  The sun's all-ripening wing
Fans up the wanton spring.
O let us both go chaunt it!
O how fresh May doth flaunt it!

Then with reports most sprightly
Trip with thy voice most lightly:
O sing, O sing, so wittily,
For now, for now, the cuckoo sings,
Cuckoo, cuckoo!
That echo doth rebound
And dally with the sound.

[1] MS. "at."

From THOMAS MORLEY'S *The
First Book of Airs*, 1600.

COME, Sorrow, come, sit down and mourn with me;
Hang down thy head upon thy baleful breast,
That God and man and all the world may see
Our heavy hearts do live in quiet rest:
Enfold thine arms and wring thy wretched hands
To shew the state wherein poor Sorrow stands.

Cry not outright, for that were children's guise,
But let thy tears fall trickling down thy face,
And weep so long until thy blubbered eyes
May see in sum[1] the depth of thy disgrace.
Oh shake thy head, but not a word but mum;
The heart once dead, the tongue is stroken dumb.

And let our fare be dishes of despite
To break our hearts and not our fasts withal;
Then let us sup with sorrow-sops at night,
And bitter sauce all of a broken gall:
Thus let us live till heavens may rue to see
The doleful doom ordained for thee and me.

From JOHN DOWLAND'S *Second
Book of Songs or Airs*, 1600.

COME, ye heavy states of night,
Do my father's spirit right;
Soundings baleful let me borrow,
Burthening my song with sorrow.
    Come, Sorrow, come! her eyes that sings
    By thee are turned into springs.

[1] Old ed. "May see (in Sunne)."

Come, you virgins of the night,
That in dirges sad delight,
Quire my anthems : I do borrow
Gold nor pearl, but sounds of sorrow.
 Come, Sorrow, come! her eyes that sings
 By thee are turned into springs.

From RICHARD CARLTON'S
Madrigals, 1601.

CONTENT thyself with thy estate,
 Seek not to climb above the skies,
For often love is mixed with hate
 And 'twixt the flowers the serpent lies :
Where fortune sends her greatest joys,
There once possest they are but toys.

What thing can earthly pleasure give
 That breeds delight when it is past?
Or who so quietly doth live
 But storms of care do drown at last?
This is the loan of worldly hire,
The more we have the more desire.

Wherefore I hold him best at ease
 That lives content with his estate,
And doth not sail in worldly seas
 Where Mine and Thine do breed debate :
This noble mind, even in a clown,
Is more than to possess a crown.

From THOMAS BATESON'S *Second
Set of Madrigals*, 1618.

CUPID, in a bed of roses
    Sleeping, chanced to be stung
    Of a bee that lay among
The flowers where he himself reposes;
And thus to his mother weeping
    Told that he this wound did take
    Of a little winged snake,
As he lay securely sleeping.
Cytherea smiling said
    That "if so great sorrow spring
    From a silly bee's weak sting
As should make thee thus dismay'd,
What anguish feel they, think'st thou, and what pain,
Whom thy empoison'd arrows cause complain?"

From *Christ Church MS.* I. 5. 49.
(Music by ALFONSO FERRA-
BOSCO.)

DAPHNIS came on a summer's day
    Where fair Phillis sleeping lay,
With breast half naked bare:
He ran and gathered stores of lilies,
Wherewith he covered his fair Phillis,
She being nought aware.
Fond youth, why dost thou mar
Those lily-bowers and lose the pain?
Her lily breast doth stain
All flowers and lilies far.

> From STAFFORD SMITH'S *Musica
> Antiqua*. (Words by
> THOMAS MAY?)

DEAR, do not your fair beauty wrong
   In thinking still you are too young;
The rose and lily in your cheek
Flourish, and no more ripening seek;
Inflaming beams shot from your eye
Do show Love's Midsummer is nigh;
Your cherry lip, red, soft, and sweet,
Proclaims such fruit for taste is meet;
Love is still young, a buxom boy,
And younglings are allowed to toy:
Then lose no time, for love hath wings,
And flies away from aged things.

> From JOHN COPERARIO'S *Funeral
> Tears*, 1606.

DECEITFUL fancy, why delud'st thou me,
   The dead alive presenting?
My joy's fair image carved in shades I see:
   O false, yet sweet, contenting!
Why art not thou a substance like to me,
Or I a shade to vanish hence with thee?

Stay, gentle object! my sense still deceive
    With this thy kind illusion;
I die through madness if my thoughts you leave:
    O strange, yet sweet, confusion!
Poor blissless heart that feels such deep annoy,
Only to lose the shadow of thy joy!

        From ROBERT JONES' *Second
        Book of Airs*, 1601.

DID ever man thus love as I!
    I think I was made
    For no other trade;
My mind doth it so hard apply,
And all fond courses else doth fly.

Undoing were a petty care;
    Losing my best hopes
    In their largest scopes,
To loving when I do compare,
Methinks I could as trifles spare.

All my sad thoughts, though wide begun,
    In her still do meet
    Who makes thinking sweet,
And then to me again they run
To tell me all that they have done.

Thus do I spend my days and hours
    In a pleasant round
    Where true joys are found,
And there alone my soul devours
All love's dear food with longing powers.

> A heav'n on earth is love well met;
> There is more content
> Than can well be spent,
> When in two fruitful hearts 'tis set
> Which will not be in either's debt.

From JOHN DOWLAND'S *A Pilgrim's Solace*, 1612.

DISDAIN me still that I may ever love,
  For who his love enjoys can love no more:
The war once past, with ease men cowards prove,
And ships returned do rot upon the shore:
And though thou frown, I'll say thou art most fair,
And still I'll love, though still I must despair.

As heat to life, so is desire to love,
And these once quenched both life and love are gone:
Let not my sighs nor tears thy Virtue move,
Like baser metals do not melt too soon:
Laugh at my woes although I ever mourn;
Love surfeits with reward, his nurse is scorn.

From ROBERT JONES' *Ultimum Vale*, 1608.

DISDAIN, that so doth fill me,
  Hath surely sworn to kill me,
  And I must die;

Desire that so doth burn me
To life again will turn me,
   And live must I.
O kill me then, disdain,
That I may live again!

Thy looks are life unto me
And yet thy looks undo me:
   O death and life!
Thy smile[1] some rest doth show me,
Thy frown with war o'erthrow me:
   O peace and strife!
Nor life nor death is either:
Then give me both or neither.

Life only cannot please[2] me,
Death only cannot ease me:
   Change is delight.
I live that death may kill me,
I die that life may fill me,
   Both day and night.
If once despair decay
Desire will wear away.

---

[1] This is the reading in Davison's *Poetical Rhapsody*, ed. 1608, and Martin Peerson's *Private Music*, 1620.—Jones gives "Thy smiles some rest do show me" and in the next line "Thy frowns."

[2] Jones reads "ease me" in this line and "please me" in the next. I have followed Davison's and Peerson's text.

From Robert Jones' *Ultimum Vale*, 1608.

Do not, O do not prize thy beauty at too high a rate,
    Love to be loved whilst thou art lovely, lest thou
        love too late ;
    Frowns print wrinkles in thy brows
    At which spiteful age doth smile,
    Women in their froward vows
    Glorying to beguile.

Wert thou the only world's admired thou canst love
        but one,
And many have before been loved, thou art not loved
        alone :
    Couldst thou speak with heavenly grace,
    Sappho might with thee compare ;
    Blush the roses in thy face,
    Rosamond was as fair.

Pride is the canker that consumeth beauty in her prime,
They that delight in long debating feel the curse of
        time :
    All things with the time do change,
    That will not the time obey ;
    Some even to themselves seem strange
    Thorough their own delay.

From ALFONSO FERRABOSCO'S
Airs, 1609.

DROWN not with tears, my dearest Love,
　Those eyes which my affections move;
Do not with weeping those lights blind
Which me in thy subjection bind.
Time that hath made us two of one,
And forced thee now to live alone,
Will once again us re-unite
To show how she can Fortune spite.
Then will we our time redeem,
And hold our hours in more esteem,
Turning all our sweetest nights
Into millions of delights;
And strive with many thousand kisses
To multiply exchange of blisses.

From ALFONSO FERRABOSCO'S
Airs, 1609.

FAIN I would, but oh I dare not,
　Speak my thoughts at full to praise her:
"Speak the best," cries Love, "and spare not;
　Thy speech can no higher raise her:
Thy speech than thy thoughts are lower,
Yet thy thoughts doth not half know her."

> From THOMAS CAMPION'S *Two
> Books of Airs* (circ. 1613).

FAIN would I my love disclose,
    Ask what honour might deny ;
But both love and her I lose,
From my motion[1] if she fly.
Worse than pain is fear to me :
Then hold in fancy though it burn !
If not happy, safe I'll be
And to my cloistered cares return.

Yet, oh yet, in vain I strive
To repress my schooled desire ;
More and more the flames revive,
I consume in mine own fire.
She would pity, might she know
The harms that I for her endure.
Speak then ! and get comfort so :
A wound long hid grows past recure.

Wise she is and needs must know
All th' attempts that beauty moves ;
Fair she is and honoured so,
That she, sure, hath tried some loves.
If with love I tempt her then,
'Tis but her due to be desired :
What would women think of men
If their deserts were not admired ?

[1] Proposal.

Women courted have the hand
To discard what they distaste;
But those dames whom none demand
Want oft what their wills embrace.
Could their firmness iron excel,
As they are fair, they should be sought;
When true thieves use falsehood well,
As they are wise, they will be caught.

From THOMAS BATESON'S *First Set of English Madrigals*, 1604.

FAIR Hebe, when dame Flora meets,
　　She trips and leaps as gallants do;
Up to the hills and down again
　　To the vallies runs she to and fro.
But out, alas! when frosty locks
　　Begirds the head with cark and care,
Peace! laugh no more, let pranks go by
　　Slow-crawling age forbids such ware.

From MICHAEL ESTE'S *Madrigals*, 1604.

FAIR is my love, my dear and only jewel,
　　Mild are her looks, but yet her heart is cruel:
O that her heart were, as her looks are, mild!
Then should I not from comfort be exiled.

From ORLANDO GIBBONS' *First Set of Madrigals*, 1612.

FAIR is the rose, yet fades with heat or cold;
Sweet are the violets, yet soon grown old;
The lily's white, yet in one day 'tis done;
White is the snow, yet melts against the sun:
So white, so sweet, was my fair mistress' face,
Yet alter'd quite in one short hour's[1] space:
So short-lived beauty a vain gloss doth borrow,
Breathing delight to-day but none to-morrow.

From ROBERT JONES' *Second Book of Songs and Airs*, 1601.

FAIR women like fair jewels are
  Whose worth lies in opinion;
To praise them all must be his care
  Who goes about to win one;
And when he hath her once obtained,
  To her face he must her flatter,
But not to others, lest he move
  Their eyes to level at her.

The way to purchase truth in love,
  If such way there be any,
Must be to give her leave to rove,
  And hinder one by many;

---

[1] "Hour" is here (as frequently in the Elizabethan poets) to be pronounced as a dissyllable. In fact it was commonly spelt "hower."

Believe thou must that she is true,[1]
  When poisoned tongues do sting her;
Rich jewels bear the self-same hue
  Worn upon any finger.

The perfectest of mind and shape
  Must look for defamations;
Live how they will, they cannot 'scape,
  Their persons are temptations:
Then let the world condemn my choice,
  As laughing at my folly;
If she be kind, the self-same voice
  Is spread of the most holy.

From ROBERT JONES' *First Book of Songs and Airs*, 1601.

FAREWELL, dear love! since thou wilt needs be gone:
Mine eyes do show my life is almost done.
    —Nay I will never die,
    So long as I can spy;
    There be many mo
    Though that she do go.
There be many mo, I fear not;
Why, then, let her go, I care not.—

Farewell, farewell! since this I find is true,
I will not spend more time in wooing you.
    —But I will seek elsewhere
    If I may find her there.

[1] Old ed. "fayre."

Shall I bid her go?
What and if I do?
Shall I bid her go and spare not?
O no, no, no, no, I dare not.—

Ten thousand times farewell! yet stay awhile.
Sweet, kiss me once, sweet kisses time beguile.
    —I have no power to move:
    How now, am I in love!—
    Wilt thou needs be gone?
    Go then, all is one.
Wilt thou needs be gone? Oh hie thee!
Nay; stay, and do no more deny me.

Once more farewell! I see *Loth to depart*[1]
Bids oft adieu to her that holds my heart:
    But seeing I must lose
    Thy love which I did choose,
    Go thy ways for me,
    Since it may not be:
Go thy ways for me! but whither?
Go,—oh but where I may come thither.

What shall I do? my love is now departed,
She is as fair as she is cruel-hearted:
    She would not be entreated
    With prayers oft repeated.
    If she come no more,
    Shall I die therefore?
If she come no more, what care I?
—Faith, let her go, or come, or tarry!

---

[1] There was an old song with this title.—See Chappell's *Popular Music of the Olden Time*, p. 173.

> From ROBERT JONES' *Second Book
> of Songs and Airs*, 1601.

FIE, fie, fie! what a coil is here!
   Why, strive you to get a kiss?
Do, do, do, what you will,
You shall be ne'er the near.[1]
Had I been willing
So to be billing,
You had prevailed long ere this:
Sweet, stand away, let me alone,
Or else in faith I'll get me gone.

Come, come, come! do you not perceive
I am not yet disposed to yield?
Stay, stay, stay but a while:
My love will give you leave.
This my denial
Is but a trial
If faint desire will fly the field.
Whoop! look you now, I pray be still:
Nay, then, in faith, do what you will.

> From JOHN DOWLAND'S *Third
> Book of Songs or Airs*, 1603.

FLOW not so fast ye fountains:
   What needeth all this haste?
Swell not above your mountains,
Nor spend your time in waste.
    Gentle springs, freshly your salt tears
    Must still fall, dropping from their spheres.

---

[1] "Ne'er the near"—never the nearer. (A proverbial expression.)

Weep they apace, whom Reason
Or lingering Time can ease:
My sorrow can no season,
Nor ought besides appease.
  Gentle springs, freshly your salt tears
  Must still fall, dropping from their spheres.

Time can abate the terror
Of every common pain :
But common grief is error,
True grief will still remain.
  Gentle springs, freshly your salt tears
  Must still fall, dropping from their spheres.

From CAMPION *and* ROSSETER'S
Book of Airs, 1601.

FOLLOW thy fair sun, unhappy shadow!
 Though thou be black as night,
 And she made all of light,
Yet follow thy fair sun, unhappy shadow!

Follow her, whose light thy light depriveth!
 Though here thou liv'st disgraced,
 And she in heaven is placed,
Yet follow her whose light the world reviveth!

Follow those pure beams, whose beauty burneth!
 That so have scorched thee
 As thou still black must be
Till her kind beams thy black to brightness turneth.

Follow her, while yet her glory shineth!
   There comes a luckless night
   That will dim all her light;
And this the black unhappy shade divineth.

Follow still, since so thy fates ordained!
   The sun must have his shade,
   Till both at once do fade,
The sun still proved,[1] the shadow still disdained.

From THOMAS BATESON'S Second
Set of Madrigals, 1618.

FOND Love is blind, blind therefore lovers be,
   But I more blind who ne'er my love did see;
Pigmalion loved an image, I a name,
I laughed at him but now deserve like blame:
Thus foolishly I leap before I look,
Seeing no bait I swallowed have the hook.

Ah Cupid grant that I may never see
Her, though mine ear that thus hath wounded me:
If through mine eyes another wound she give,
Cupid, alas! then I no longer live,
But die, poor wretch, shot through and through the liver
With those sharp arrows she stole from thy quiver.

[1] *i.e.*, approved.

From Dr. John Wilson's *Cheerful Airs or Ballads*, 1660.

FONDNESS of man to love a she,
    Were beauty's image on her face
So carved by immortality
    As envious time cannot disgrace.

Who shall weigh a lover's pain?
    Feigned smiles awhile his hopes may steer;
But soon reduced by sad disdain
    To the first principles of fear.

Then farewell, fairest, ne'er will I
    Pursue uncertain blisses more:
Who sails by woman's constancy,
    Shipwracks his love on every shore.

From John Dowland's *A Pilgrim's Solace*, 1612.

GO, nightly cares, the enemy to rest,
    Forbear awhile to vex my wearied sprite;
So long your weight hath lain upon my breast
That, lo.! I live of life bereaved quite:
O give me time to draw my wearied breath,
Or let me die as I desire the death.
Welcome, sweet Death! O life, no life, a hell!
Then thus and thus I bid the world farewell.

False world, farewell, the enemy to rest,
Now do thy worst, I do not weigh thy spite ;
Free from thy cares I live for ever blest,
Enjoying peace and heavenly true delight :
Delight, whom woes nor sorrows shall amate,
Nor fears or tears disturb her happy state :
And thus I leave thy hopes, thy joys untrue,
And thus, and thus, vain world, again adieu !

From Dr. John Wilson's *Cheer-
ful Airs or Ballads,* 1660.

GREEDY lover, pause awhile,
   And remember that a smile
      Heretofore
Would have made thy hopes a feast ;
      Which is more,
Since thy diet was increased,
Than both looks and language too,
Or the face itself, can do.

Such a province is my hand
As, if it thou couldst command,
      Heretofore
There thy lips would seem to dwell ;
      Which is more,
Ever since they sped so well,
Than they can be brought to do
By my neck and bosom too.

If the centre of my breast,
A dominion unpossest
    Heretofore,
May thy wandering thoughts suffice,
    Seek no more,
And my heart shall be thy prize :
So thou keep above the line,
All the hemisphere is thine.

If the flames of love were pure,
Which by oath thou didst assure
    Heretofore,
Gold that goes into the clear
    Shines the more
When it leaves again the fire :
Let not then those looks of thine
Blemish what they should refine.

I have cast into the fire
Almost all thou couldst desire
    Heretofore ;
But I see thou art to crave
    More and more.
Should I cast in all I have,
So that I were ne'er so free,
Thou wouldst burn, though not for me.

From THOMAS CAMPION'S *Two Books of Airs* (circ. 1613).

HARDEN now thy tired heart with more than flinty rage!
Ne'er let her false tears henceforth thy constant grief assuage!
Once true happy days thou saw'st, when she stood firm and kind;
Both as one then lived, and held one ear, one tongue, one mind:
But now those bright hours be fled and never may return:
What then remains but her untruths to mourn!

Silly trait'ress, who shall now thy careless tresses place?
Who thy pretty talk supply? whose ear thy music grace?
Who shall thy bright eyes admire, what lips triumph with thine?
Day by day who'll visit thee and say "Th' art only mine."
Such a time there was, God wot, but such shall never be.
Too oft, I fear, thou wilt remember me.

From CAMPION and ROSSETER'S
Book of Airs, 1601.

HARK, all you ladies that do sleep !
  The fairy-queen Proserpina
Bids you awake and pity them that weep :
  You may do in the dark
    What the day doth forbid ;
  Fear not the dogs that bark,
    Night will have all hid.

But if you let your lovers moan,
  The fairy-queen Proserpina
Will send abroad her fairies every one,
  That shall pinch black and blue
    Your white hands and fair arms
  That did not kindly rue
    Your paramours'[1] harms.

In myrtle arbours on the downs
  The fairy-queen Proserpina,
This night by moonshine leading merry rounds,
  Holds a watch with sweet love,
    Down the dale, up the hill ;
  No plaints or groans may move
    Their holy vigil.

---

[1] "Paramour"=lover. (The word acquired its present offensive meaning at a later date.)

All you that will hold watch with love,
    The fairy-queen Proserpina
Will make you fairer than Dione's dove ;
    Roses red, lilies white,
        And the clear damask hue,
    Shall on your cheeks alight :
        Love will adorn you.

All you that love or loved before,
    The fairy-queen Proserpina
Bids you increase that loving humour more :
    They that yet have not fed
        On delight amorous,
    She vows that they shall lead
        Apes in Avernus.

From *Pammelia*, 1609.

HEIGH ho !
    To the greenwood now let us go !
Sing heave and ho !
And there shall we find both buck and doe :
Sing heave and ho !
The hart and hind and the pretty little roe.
Sing heave and ho !

From Thomas Campion's *Fourth
Book of Airs* (circ. 1617).

Her fair inflaming eyes,
  Chief authors of my cares,
I prayed in humblest wise
  With grace to view my tears:
They beheld me broad awake,
But alas no ruth would take.

Her lips with kisses rich,
  And words of fair delight,
I fairly did beseech
  To pity my sad plight:
But a voice from them broke forth,
As a whirlwind from the north.

Then to her hands I fled,
  That can give heart and all;
To them I long did plead,
  And loud for pity call:
But, alas, they put me off
With a touch worse than a scoff.

So back I straight return'd,
  And at her breast I knock'd,
Where long in vain I mourn'd,
  Her heart so fast was lock'd:
Not a word could passage find,
For a rock enclosed her mind.

Then down my prayers made way
  To those most comely parts
That make her fly or stay,
  As they affect deserts :
But her angry feet, thus moved,
Fled with all the parts I loved.

Yet fled they not so fast
  As her enraged mind :
Still did I after haste,
  Still was I left behind ;
Till I found 'twas to no end
With a spirit to contend.

From THOMAS BATESON'S Second
Set of Madrigals, 1618.

HER hair the net of golden wire,
  Wherein my heart, led by my wandering eyes,
So fast entangled is that in no wise
It can, nor will, again retire ;
But rather will in that sweet bondage die
Than break one hair to gain her liberty.

From Christ Church MS. 1. 5. 49.

HEY nonny no !
  Men are fools that wish to die !
Is't not fine to dance and sing
When the bells of death do ring ?

Is't not fine to swim in wine,
And turn upon the toe
And sing hey nonny no,
When the winds blow and the seas flow?
Hey nonny no!

Finis.   Mr. Gyles.

From *MS. Mus. Sch. F.* 575.

HOLD, cruel Love, O hold! I yield.
   Withhold thy fatal dart!
This is a chamber, not a field,
   No place to strike a heart.
So oft thou hast my bosom cleft,
   So oft destroyed this park,
That all the harts that here are left
   Scarce makes another mark.

From Thomas Campion's *Two Books of Airs* (circ. 1613).

HOW eas'ly wert thou chained,
   Fond heart, by favours feigned!
Why lived thy hopes in grace,
Straight to die disdained?
But since thou'rt now beguiled
By love that falsely smiled,
In some less happy place
Mourn alone exiled.
My love still here increaseth,
And with my love my grief,

While her sweet bounty ceaseth,
That gave my woes relief.
Yet 'tis no woman leaves me,
For such may prove unjust :
A goddess thus deceives me !
Whose faith who could mistrust ?

A goddess so much graced
That Paradise is placed
In her most heav'nly breast,
Once by Love embraced.
But Love, that so kind proved,
Is now from her removed ;
Nor will he longer rest
Where no faith is loved.
If powers celestial wound us
And will not yield relief,
Woe then must needs confound us,
For none can cure our grief.
No wonder if I languish
Through burden of my smart :
It is no common anguish
From Paradise to part.

From ROBERT JONES' *The Muses
Garden of Delights*, 1610.

HOW many new years have grown old
Since first your servant old was new !
How many long hours have I told
Since first my love was vowed to you !
And yet, alas ! she doth not know
Whether her servant love or no.

How many walls as white as snow,
And windows clear as any glass,
Have I conjured to tell you so,
Which faithfully performed was!
And yet you'll swear you do not know
Whether your servant love or no.

How often hath my pale lean face,
With true characters of my love,
Petitioned to you for grace,
Whom neither sighs nor tears can move!
O cruel, yet do you not know
Whether your servant love or no?

And wanting oft a better token,
I have been fain to send my heart,
Which now your cold disdain hath broken,
Nor can you heal't by any art:
O look upon't, and you shall know
Whether your servant love or no?

From CAMPION and ROSSETER'S
Book of Airs, 1601.

I CARE not for these ladies
  That must be wooed and prayed,
Give me kind Amaryllis,
  The wanton country maid:
Nature art disdaineth,
Her beauty is her own:
    Her when we court and kiss,
    She cries "Forsooth, let go!"
    But when we come where comfort is,
    She never will say "No."

If I love Amaryllis,
  She gives me fruit and flowers;
But if we love these ladies,
  We must give golden showers.
Give them gold that sell love,
Give me the nut-brown lass,
    Who when we court and kiss,
    She cries "Forsooth, let go!"
    But when we come where comfort is,
    She never will say "No."

These ladies must have pillows
  And beds by strangers wrought;
Give me a bower of willows,
  Of moss and leaves unbought;
And fresh Amaryllis,
With milk and honey fed,
    Who when we court and kiss,
    She cries "Forsooth, let go!"
    But when we come where comfort is,
    She never will say "No."

From THOMAS BATESON'S Second
Set of Madrigals, 1618.

I HEARD a noise and wished for a sight,
  I looked aside and did a shadow see,
Whose substance was the sum of my delight:
  It came unseen and so it went from me,
But yet conceit persuaded my intent
There was a substance where the shadow went.

I did not play Narcissus in conceit,
  I did not see my shadow in a spring,
I knew my eyes were dimm'd with no deceit,
  I saw the shadow of some worthy thing;
For, as I saw the shadow passing by,
  I had a glance of something in my eye:
Shadow or she, or both, or chuse you whether,
Blessed be the thing that brought the shadow hether!

From JOHN BARTLET'S *Airs*
1606.

I HEARD of late that Love was fall'n asleep;
  Too late, alas! I find it was not so:
Methought I saw the little villain weep,
  But thief! he laughs at them that wail in woe:
I dream'd his bow was broke and he was slain,
But lo! awaked, I see all whole again.

His blinking eyes will ever be awake,
  His idle head is full of laughing toys,
His bow and shafts are tickle things to take,
  It is no meddling with such apish boys;
For they shall find, that in his fetters fall,
Love is a deadly thing to deal withal.

Yet where the wretch doth take a happy vein,
  It is the kindest worm that ever was;
But let him catch a coy conceit again,
  In frantic fits he doth a fury pass:
So that, in sum, who hopes of happy joy,
Take heed of Love, it is a parlous boy.

>From ROBERT JONES' *Musical
Dream*, 1609.

I KNOW not what, yet that I feel is much ;
   It came I know not when, it was not ever ;
Yet hurts I know not how, yet is it such
   As I am pleased though it be cured never :
It is a wound that wasteth still in woe,
And yet I would not that it were not so.

Pleased with a thought that endeth with a sigh,
   Sometimes I smile when tears stand in my eyes,
Yet then and there such sweet contentment lieth
   Both when and where my sweet sour torment lies :
O, out alas ! I cannot long endure it,
And yet, alas ! I care not when I cure it.

But, well-a-way, methinks I am not she
   That wonted was these fits as foul to scorn :
One and the same, even so I seem to be,
   As lost I live, yet of myself forlorn.
What may this be that thus my mind doth move ?
Alas ! I fear,—God shield it be not love !

>From THOMAS CAMPION'S *Fourth
Book of Airs* (circ. 1617).

I MUST complain, yet do enjoy my love ;
   She is too fair, too rich in lovely parts :
Thence is my grief, for Nature, while she strove
   With all her graces and divinest arts
To form her too too beautiful of hue,
She had no leisure left to make her true.

Should I, aggrieved, then wish she were less fair?
  That were repugnant to my own desires.
She is admired, new lovers still repair,
  That kindles daily love's forgetful fires.
Rest, jealous thoughts, and thus resolve at last,—
She hath more beauty than becomes the chaste.

From JOHN DANYEL'S *Songs for the Lute, Viol and Voice*, 1606.

IF I could shut the gate against my thoughts
  And keep out sorrow from this room within,
Or memory could cancel all the notes
  Of my misdeeds, and I unthink my sin:
How free, how clear, how clean my soul should lie,
Discharged of such a loathsome company!

Or were there other rooms without my heart
  That did not to my conscience join so near,
Where I might lodge the thoughts of sin apart
  That I might not their clam'rous crying hear;
What peace, what joy, what ease should I possess,
Freed from their horrors that my soul oppress!

But, O my Saviour, who my refuge art,
  Let thy dear mercies stand 'twixt them and me,
And be the wall to separate my heart
  So that I may at length repose me free;
That peace, and joy, and rest may be within,
And I remain divided from my sin.

From THOMAS BATESON'S *Second
Set of Madrigals*, 1618. (Compared with *Christ Church
MS.*, I. 5. 49.)

IF I seek to enjoy the fruits of my pain,
She careless denies me with words of disdain ;[1]
Yet so must I love her
That nothing can ease[2] me or move her.
Alas, why contend I, why strive I in vain,
The water to mingle
With oil that is frail[3] and loves to be single?

'Tis not Love but Fate, whose doom I abide.
You powers and you planets which destinies guide,
Change your opposition ;
It fits heavenly powers to be mild of condition.
You[4] only can alter her scorn[5] and her pride
Who me now disdaineth :
For women can tell when the right planet reigneth.

[1] "With words of disdain" is the reading of the MS.—Bateson gives "with endles disdaine."
[2] So MS.—Bateson "can either remoue me or moue her."
[3] So MS.—Bateson "ayre."
[4] Bateson omits the last three verses.
[5] MS. "storme."

> From WILLIAM BYRD'S *Songs of
> Sundry Natures*, 1589.

IF in thine heart thou nourish ill,
    And give all to thy lust,
Then sorrows sharp and griefs at length
    Endure of force thou must :
But if that reason rule thy will,
    And govern all thy mind,
A blessed life then shalt thou lead
    And fewest dangers find.

> From THOMAS CAMPION'S *Third
> Book of Airs* (circ. 1617).

IF love loves truth then women do not love,
    Their passions all are but dissembled shows :
Now kind and free of favour if they prove,
Their kindness straight a tempest overthrows.
Then as a seaman the poor lover fares ;
The storm drowns him ere he can drown his cares.

But why accuse I women that deceive ?
Blame then the foxes for their subtle wile !
They first from Nature did their craft receive ;
It is a woman's nature to beguile.
Yet some, I grant, in loving steadfast grow ;
But such by use are made, not Nature, so.

O why had Nature power at once to frame
Deceit and Beauty, traitors both to Love?
O would Deceit had died when Beauty came
With her divineness every heart to move!
Yet do we rather wish, whate'er befall,
To have fair women false than none at all.

From CAMPION and ROSSETER'S
Book of Airs, 1601.

IF she forsake me, I must die:
   Shall I tell her so?
Alas, then straight will she reply
   "No, no, no, no, no!"
If I disclose my desperate state,
She will but make sport thereat,
   And more unrelenting grow.

What heart can long such pains abide?
   Fie upon this love!
I would adventure far and wide,
   If it would remove;
But love will still my steps pursue,
I cannot his ways eschew:
   Thus still helpless hopes I prove.

I do my love in lines commend,
   But, alas, in vain;
The costly gifts that I do send,
   She returns again:
Thus still is my despair procured,
And her malice more assured:
   Then come, death, and end my pain!

From *MS, Mus. Sch. F.* 575.

IF when I die, to Hell's eternal shade
    As an idolater condemned I be,
Because a mortal beauty that doth fade
    I have too long adored in cruel thee;
Think not to scape, for, for thy tyranny,
Thou there shalt be condemned as well as I.

From RICHARD CARLTON'S *Madrigals,* 1601.

IF women can be courteous when they list,
    And when they list disdainful and unkind;
If they can bear affection in their fist
    And sell their love as they the market find;
'Twere not amiss, while Smithfield fair doth hold,
That jades and drabs together all were sold.

From JOHN ATTEY'S *First Book of Airs,* 1622.

IN a grove of trees of myrtle
    Venus met fair Myrrha's child:
"Kiss," quoth she, "my pretty turtle!"
    But her hopes he did beguile
With "No, no, no, no, no, no, no!"

"Come, O come, my dearest treasure,
 And look babies[1] in my eyes :
Cull and kiss, enjoy thy pleasure : "
 But her kindness he denies
With " No, no, no, no, no, no, no !"

" Loutish lad, come learn to venture
 On the ivory breast of love,
I dare stay the worst encounter : "
 But her words as wind did prove,
With " No, no, no, no, no, no, no !"

" Shall then love be thus abused
 By the beauty of a boy?
Shall my temple be refused,
 Will Adonis still be coy
With ' No, no, no, no, no, no, no ? '

" Then I vow that beauty ever
 Shall neglected be of love ;
Let the foolish boy persever,
 He the folly now shall prove
Of ' No, no, no, no, no, no, no ! ' "

From WILLIAM BYRD'S *Psalms, Sonnets, and Songs,* 1588.

IN fields abroad, where trumpets shrill do sound,
 Where glaives and shields do give and take the knocks,
Where bodies dead do overspread the ground,
 And friends to foes are common butchers' blocks ;

---

[1] "Look babies in the eyes,"—peer amorously in a mistress' eyes.

A gallant shot, well managing his piece,
In my conceit deserves a golden fleece.

Amid the seas a gallant ship set out,
   Wherein nor men nor yet munition lacks,
In greatest winds that spareth not a clout,
   But cuts the waves in spite of weather's wracks,
Would force a swain that comes of cowards' kind
To change himself and be of noble mind.

Who makes his seat a stately stamping steed,
   Whose neighs and plays are princely to behold,
Whose courage stout, whose eyes are fiery red,
   Whose joints well-knit, whose harness all of gold,
Doth well deserve to be no meaner thing
Than Persian knight whose horse made him a king.

By that bedside where sits a gallant dame,
   Who casteth off her brave and rich attire,
Whose petticoat sets forth as fair a frame
   As mortal men or gods can well desire;
Who sits and sees her petticoat unlaced,—
I say no more, the rest are all disgraced.

From MARTIN PEERSON'S *Pri
vate Music*, 1620.

He.[1] IS not that my fancy's Queen,
   In the brightness of her rays
   Passing summer's cheerest days,
That comes tripping o'er the green?

[1] There are no prefixes in old ed.

She. Is[1] not that my shepherd swain
      Sprightly clad in lovely blue,
      Fairest of the fairest crew,
   That comes gliding o'er the plain?

Both. It is my love, it is my love,
      And thus and thus we meet,
      And thus and thus we greet,
   Happier than the gods above:
   Meeting may we love for ever,
   Ever love and never sever!

From CAMPION and ROSSETER'S
Book of Airs, 1601.

IT fell on a summer's day,
  While sweet Bessy sleeping lay,
In her bower, on her bed,
Light with curtains shadowed,
Jamy came: she him spies,
Opening half her heavy eyes.

Jamy stole in through the door,
She lay slumb'ring as before;
Softly to her he drew near,
She heard him, yet would not hear:
Bessy vowed not to speak,
He resolved that dump to break.

---

[1] The second stanza is printed in old ed. as part of another song.

First a soft kiss he doth take,
She lay still and would not wake ;
Then his hands learn'd to woo,
She dreamt not what he would do,
But still slept, while he smiled
To see love by sleep beguiled.

Jamy then began to play,
Bessy as one buried lay,
Gladly still through this sleight
Deceived in her own deceit ;
And since this trance begoon,
She sleeps every afternoon.

From ROBERT JONES' *The Muses'
Garden of Delights*, 1610.

JOY in thy hope, the earnest of thy love,
  For so thou mayst enjoy thy heart's desire :
True hopes things absent do as present prove,
And keep alive love's still-renewing fire.

But of thy hope let silence be the tongue,
And secresy the heart of loving fire ;
For hopes revealed may thy hopes prolong
Or cut them off in prime-time of desire.

Sweet are those hopes that do themselves enjoy,
As vowed to themselves to live and die ;
Sweetest those joys and freest from annoy
That waken not the eye of jealousy.

L'Envoy.
Thy love is not thy love if not thine own,
And so it is not if it once be known.

> From JOHN FORBES' *Cantus,
> Songs and Fancies*, 1661 (compared with *Advocates' Library
> MS.* 5. 2. 14.)

JOY to the person of my love !
Altho' she me disdain,
Fixed are my thoughts and may not move ;
And yet I love in vain.
Shall I lose the sight
Of my joy and heart's delight ?
Or shall I leave my suit ?
Shall I strive to touch ?
Oh no, it were too much :
She is forbidden fruit.
Oh woe is me
That ever I did see
The beauty that did me bewitch !
Yet out, alas,
I must forego that face,
The treasure I esteemed so rich.[1]

Oh shall I range into some dale,
Or to the mountains mourn ?
Shall[2] Echo still resound my tale,
Or whither shall I turn ?

---

[1] Both Forbes and the MS. give "much."
[2] So the line stands in the MS.—Forbes gives "Sad echoes shal resound my tale."

Shall[1] I by her live
That no life to me will give
But deeply wounds my heart?
If[2] I fly away,
Oh will she not cry "Stay,
Thy sorrows I'll convert"?
Oh no, no, no,
She will not once say so;
But comfortless I must be gone.
Yet altho'[3] she be
So froward[4] unto me,
I'll love her or I will[5] love none.

Oh that I might but understand
The causes[6] of her hate
To him would[7] be at her command
In love, in life, in state!
Then should I no more
In heart be grieved so sore,
Nor fed with discontent.
But since that I have loved

---

[1] "Shall I .. give." This is the reading of the MS. Forbes reads:—

"Shall I buy that love
No life to me will give," &c.

The line "But deeply wounds my heart" is omitted in the MS.

[2] "If I fly .. convert." So the MS. Forbes reads:—

"If I flee away
She will not to me say stay
My sorrows to convert."

[3] So the MS.—Forbes "tho'."
[4] So the MS.—Forbes "thrawart."
[5] So the MS.—Forbes "shal."
[6] So the MS.—Forbes "reasons."
[7] So Forbes.—MS. "him that would be."

A maid that hath me proved [1]
Unworthy, I do repent.
Something unkind
Hath settled in her mind,
That caused her to hate me so.
Sweet saint,[2] unto me be but half so kind
As let me the occasion know.

Thousand fortunes fall to her share!
Tho' she has rejected me
And filled my heart[3] full of despair,
Yet shall I constant be;
For she is the dame
My tongue[4] shall ne'er defame,[5]
Fair branch of modesty,
Chaste of[6] heart and mind.
Oh were she half so kind,
Then would she pity me!
Sweet, turn at last;
Be kind as thou art chaste,
And let me in thy bosom dwell:
So shall we gain
The pleasure of Love's pain.
Till then, my dearest dear,[7] farewell.

[1] Forbes "that so hath prov'd."—The MS. reads:—
"A Maid that hath me prov'de,
And worthie I do" &c.
[2] "Sweet ... know." So the MS.—Forbes gives:—
"Sweet, seem to me but half so kind to be
Or let me" &c.
[3] So Forbes.—MS. "my sad heart."
[4] So Forbes.—MS. "That my tongue."
[5] "Ne'er defame" is the reading of the MS. Forbes gives
 ever name."   [6] So Forbes.—MS. "in."
[7] So the MS.—Forbes "love." (I have not noticed all the

From ORLANDO GIBBONS' *First
Set of Madrigals*, 1612.

LAIS, now old, that erst attempting[1] lass,
  To Goddess Venus consecrates her glass;
For she herself hath now no use of one,
No dimpled cheeks hath she to gaze upon:
She cannot see her springtide damask grace,
Nor dare she look upon her winter face.

From THOMAS GREAVES' *Songs
of Sundry Kinds*, 1604.

LET dread of pain for sin in after-time,
  Let shame to see thyself ensnared so,
Let grief conceived for foul accursed crime,
  Let hate of sin the worker of thy woe,
With dread, with shame, with grief, with hate enforce
To dew thy cheeks with tears of deep remorse.

So hate of sin shall cause God's love to grow,
  So grief shall harbour hope within thy heart,
So dread shall cause the flood of joy to flow,
  So shame shall send sweet solace to thy smart:
So love, so hope, so joy, so solace sweet
Shall make thy soul in heavenly bliss to fleet.[2]

various readings; but in some instances have silently followed the printed copy.)

[1] I suspect that this is a misprint for "all-tempting."
[2] Float.

Woe where such hate doth no such love allure!
Woe where such grief doth make no hope proceed!
Woe where such dread doth no such joy procure!
Woe where such shame doth no such solace breed!
Woe where no hate, no grief, no dread, no shame,
Doth neither love, hope, joy, or solace frame!

From Christ Church MS. K. 3,
43.5. (Music by Thomas
Ford.)

LET not thy blackness move thee to despair;
  Black women are beloved of men that's fair.
What if thy hair her flaxen brightness lack?
Thy face is comely though thy brow be black.

From ROBERT JONES' First Book
of Songs and Airs, 1601.

LIE down, poor heart, and die awhile for grief,
  Think not this world will ever do thee good;
Fortune forewarns thou look to thy relief,
  And sorrow sucks upon thy living blood:
Then this is all can help thee of this hell,
Lie down and die, and then thou shalt do well.

Day gives his light but to thy labours' toil,
  And night her rest but to thy weary bones;
Thy fairest fortune's[1] followed with a foil,
  And laughing ends but with thine[2] after-groans:
And this is all can help thee of thy hell,
Lie down and die, and then thou shalt do well.

---

[1] Old ed. "fortune followes."   [2] Old ed. "their."

Patience doth pine and pity ease no pain,
  Time wears the thoughts, but nothing helps the
    mind;
Dead and alive, alive and dead again,
  These are the fits that thou art like to find:
And this is all can help thee of thy hell,
Lie down and die, and then thou shalt do well.

From RICHARD CARLTON'S
Madrigals, 1601.

LIKE as the gentle heart itself bewrays
  In doing gentle deeds with frank delight,
Even so the baser mind itself displays
  In cankered malice and revengeful spite.

From MARTIN PEERSON'S Private Music, 1620. (Words by SIR PHILIP SIDNEY.)

LOCK up, fair lids, the treasure of my heart,
  Preserve those beams this age's only light;
To her sweet sense, sweet Sleep, some ease impart,
  Her sense too weak to bear her spirit's might.
And while, O sleep, thou closest up her sight,
Her sight[1] where Love doth forge his fairest dart,
  O harbour all her parts in easeful plight;
Let no strange dream make her fair body start.

[1] Old ed. "light."

But yet, O dream, if thou wilt not depart
  In this rare subject from thy common right,
  But wilt thyself in such a seat delight,
Then take my shape and play a lover's part :
Kiss her from me, and say unto her sprite,
Till her eyes shine I live in darkest night.

From MARTIN PEERSON'S *Private Music*, 1620.

LOVE her no more, herself she doth not love :
    Shame and the blackest clouds of night
  Hide her for ever from thy sight.
O day, why do thy beams in her eyes move?
    Fly her, dear honoured friend, do so ;
    She'll be the cause of much much woe.
      Alas, she will undo thee,
      Her love is fatal to thee :
  Curse her then and go !

From ROBERT JONES' *First Set of Madrigals*, 1607.

LOVE, if a God thou art,
  Then evermore thou must
Be merciful and just :
Then wherefore doth thy dart
Wound me alone and not my lady's heart ?[1]

---

[1] Only the first five lines are given in the song-book. The rest is from Davison's *Poetical Rhapsody*.

If merciful, then why
Am I to pain reserved,
That have thee truly served;
When she, that by thy power sets not a fly,
Laughs thee to scorn and lives in liberty?

Then, if a God thou wilt accounted be,
Heal me like her, or else wound her like me.

From WALTER PORTER'S *Madrigals and Airs*, 1632.

LOVE in thy youth, fair maid; be wise,
    Old Time will make thee colder,
And though each morning new arise
    Yet we each day grow older.
Thou as heaven art fair and young,
    Thine eyes like twin stars shining:
But ere another day be sprung,
    All these will be declining.
Then winter comes with all his fears
    And all thy sweets shall borrow;
Too late then wilt thou shower thy tears,
    And I too late shall sorrow.

From THOMAS CAMPION'S *Fourth Book of Airs* (circ. 1617).

LOVE me or not, love her I must or die;
    Leave me or not, follow her needs must I.
O that her grace would my wished comforts give!
How rich in her, how happy I should live!

All my desire, all my delight should be
Her to enjoy, her to unite with me ;
Envy should cease, her would I love alone :
Who loves by looks is seldom true to one.

Could I enchant, and that it lawful were,
Her would I charm softly that none should hear ;
But love enforced rarely yields firm content :
So would I love that neither should repent.

From *Add. MS.* 10, 338.

Phœbe and Endymion.

Phœbe. LOVELY shepherd, ope thine eye ;
   Sleep is loss when I stand by.
Endym. Who's that who does forbid me sleep ?
   Has the wolf dispersed my sheep ?
Phœbe. I keep thy flocks ; they feed secure and
    free :
   Would I could guard my heart as well from
    thee.
Endym. I blush to hear of love.
Phœbe.   And I
   Grieve to see thy cruelty.
Endym. As yet I have no cares, but can
   To my homely oaten reed
   Sing the praises of great Pan ;
   But love, they say, does sorrow breed.
Phœbe. Peevish lad, canst thou disdain
   The silver goddess of the night,

>   When with all her starry train
>   She comes to bring thee full delight?
>   Follow me unto my bed,
>   Or in revenge I'll kiss thee dead.
> *Endym.* I am but young, fair queen, and do not know
>   Whether there be a god of love or no.
> *Phœbe.* I'll shew thee Cupid, boy, and he
>   Every day shall play with thee;
>   But the night belongs to me.
>   Bid Latmos then adieu;
>   On that cold mount spend not thine age's prime:
>   Thou'st higher hills to climb.

> From THOMAS MORLEY'S *The First Book of Airs*, 1600.

MISTRESS mine, well may you fare!
Kind be your thoughts and void of care,
Sweet Saint Venus be your speed
That you may in love proceed.
Coll me and clip and kiss me too,
So so so so so so true love should do.

This fair morning, sunny bright,
That gives life to love's delight,
Every heart with heat inflames,
And our[1] cold affection blames.
Coll me and clip and kiss me too,
So so so so so [so] true love should do.

---
[1] Old ed. "out."

In these woods are none but birds,
They can speak but silent words ;
They are pretty harmless things,
They will shade us with their wings.
Coll me and clip and kiss me too,
So so so so so [so] true love should do.

Never strive nor make no noise,
'Tis for foolish girls and boys ;
Every childish thing can say
'Go to, how now, pray away!'
Coll me and clip and kiss me too,
So so so so so [so] true love should do.

From JOHN DOWLAND'S *Second Book of Airs*, 1600.

MOURN, mourn! day is with darkness fled !
    What heaven then governs earth ?
O none ; but hell in heaven's stead
   Chokes with his mists our mirth.
Mourn, mourn ! look now for no more day,
   Nor night but that from hell ;
Then all must, as they may,
   In darkness learn to dwell :
But yet this change must needs change our delight,
That thus the sun should harbour with the night.

> From THOMAS BATESON'S *First
> Set of English Madrigals*,
> 1604.

MUSIC, some think, no music is
Unless she sing of clip and kiss,
And bring to wanton tunes " Fie, fie ! "
Or " Tih-ha tah-ha ! " or " I'll cry ! "
But let such rhymes no more disgrace
Music sprung of heavenly race.

> From ROBERT JONES' *A Musical
> Dream*, 1609.

MY complaining is but feigning,
All my love is but in jest ;
     (Fa, la, la !)
And my courting is but sporting,
In most shewing meaning least.
     (Fa, la, la !)

Outward sadness inward gladness
Representeth in my mind ;
     (Fa, la, la !)
In most feigning most obtaining,
Such good faith in love I find.
     (Fa, la, la !)

Towards ladies this my trade is,
Two minds in one breast I wear ;
     (Fa, la, la !)
And, my measure at my pleasure,
Ice and flame my face doth bear.
     (Fa, la, la !)

From *Add. MS.* 17790. (Set to
music by WILLIAM BYRD.)

MY little sweet darling, my comfort and joy,
  (Sing lullaby, lulla !)
In beauty surpassing the princes of Troy,
  (Sing lullaby, lulla !)
Now suck, child, and sleep, child, thy mother's sweet
  boy !
  (Sing lullaby, lulla!)
The gods bless and keep thee from cruel annoy!
  Sing lulla, lulla, sweet baby,
  Lulla, lulla, sweet baby,
  Lullaby, lulla.

From THOMAS BATESON'S *Second
Set of Madrigals*, 1618.

MY mistress after service due
  Demanded if indeed my love were true.
I said it was ; then she replied,
That I must hate
Whom she defied,
And so myself above the rest,
Whom she (she swore) did most of all detest.
In sooth, said I, you see I hate myself,
Who sets my love on such a peevish elf.

> From *Christ Church MS.* K. 3.
> 43-5. (Music by THOMAS
> FORD.)

MY sins are like the hairs upon my head
   And raise their audit to as high a score.
In this they differ : *they* do daily shed,
But ah my sins grow daily more and more :
If by my hairs thou number out my sins,
Heaven make me bald before that day begins.

> From ORLANDO GIBBONS' *First
> Set of Madrigals*, 1612.

NAY, let me weep, though others' tears be spent ;
    Though all eyes dried be, let mine be wet ;
Unto thy grave I'll pay this yearly rent,
    Thy lifeless corse demands of me this debt :
I owe more tears than ever corse did crave,
I'll pay more tears than e'er was paid to grave.

Ne'er let the sun with his deceiving light
    Seek to make glad these wat'ry eyes of mine ;
My sorrow suits with melancholy night,
    I joy in dole, in languishment I pine :
My dearest friend is set, he was my sun,
With whom my mirth, my joy, and all is done.

Yet if that age had frosted o'er his head,
  Or if his face had furrow'd been with years,
I would not thus bemoan that he is dead,
  I might have been more niggard of my tears:
But O the sun new-rose is gone to bed,
And lilies in the spring-time hang their head.

From THOMAS CAMPION'S *The Description of a Masque presented before the King's Majesty at Whitehall*, 1607.

NEITHER buskin now, nor bays,
  Challenge I ; a lady's praise
Shall content my proudest hope :
Their applause was all my scope,
And to their shrines properly
Revels dedicated be :
Whose soft ears none ought to pierce
But with smooth and gentle verse.
Let the tragic poem swell,
Raising raging fiends from hell ;
And let epic dactyls range
Swelling seas and countries strange :
Little room small things contains,
Easy praise quits easy pains.
Suffer them whose brows do sweat
To gain honour by the great ;[1]
It's enough if men me name
A retailer of the same.

[1] "By the great,"—wholesale.

> From THOMAS WEELKES' *Madrigals of Five and Six Parts*, 1600.

NOELL, adieu, adieu! thou Court's delight,
    Upon whose locks the Graces sweetly played;
Now thou art dead our pleasure dies outright,
    For who can joy when thou in dust art laid?
Bedew, my notes, his death-bed with your tears,
    Time helps some grief, no time your griefs outwears.

> From JOHN DOWLAND'S *Second Book of Songs or Airs*, 1600.

NOW cease, my wand'ring eyes,
    Strange beauties to admire;
In change least comfort lies,
    Long joys yield long desire:
        One faith, one love,
Make our frail pleasures eternal and in sweetness prove;
        New hopes, new joys,
Are still with sorrow declining unto deep annoys.

    One man hath but one soul,
        Which Art cannot divide;
    If all one soul must love,
        Two loves must be denied:

    One soul, one love
By faith and merit united cannot remove :
    Distracted sprites
Are ever changing, and hapless in their delights.

  Nature two eyes hath given,
    All beauty to impart
  As well in earth as heaven,
    But she hath given one heart ;
    That though we see
Ten thousand beauties, yet in us One should be,
    One steadfast love,
Because our hearts stand fixt although our eyes do
  move.

       From THOMAS ROBINSON'S *New*
        Cithern Lessons, 1609.

NOW, Cupid, look about thee,
  Thy kingdom is decaying ;
Young men begin to flout thee,
  And turn their deeds to saying :
In men there is no passion,
Love is so out of fashion.

> From THOMAS CAMPION'S *The Description of a Masque presented before the King's Majesty at Whitehall*, 1607.

NOW hath Flora robbed her bowers
  To befriend this place with flowers :
    Strow about, strow about !
The sky rained never kindlier showers.
Flowers with bridals well agree,
Fresh as brides and bridegrooms be.
    Strow about, strow about !
And mix them with fit melody.
Earth hath no princelier flowers
Than roses white and roses red,
But they must still be mingled :
And as a rose new plucked from Venus' thorn,
So doth a bride her bridegroom's bed adorn.

Divers divers flowers affect
For some private dear respect :
    Strow about, strow about !
Let every one his own protect,
But he's none of Flora's friend
That will not the rose commend.
    Strow about, strow about !
Let princes princely flowers defend :
Roses, the garden's pride,
Are flowers for love and flowers for kings,
In courts desired and weddings :
And as a rose in Venus' bosom worn,
So doth a bridegroom his bride's bed adorn.

> From Francis Pilkington's
> *First Book of Songs or Airs,*
> 1605.

NOW peep, bo-peep, thrice happy blest mine eyes !
For I have found fair Phillis where she lies,
    Upon her bed
    With arms unspread,
        All fast asleep ;
    Unmask'd her face,
    Thrice happy grace !
        Farewell, my sheep :
Look to yourselves, new charge I must approve,
Phyllis doth sleep and I must guard my love.

Now peep, bo-peep, mine eyes to see your bliss,
Phillis' closed eyes attracts you her [1] to kiss.
    O may I now
    Perform my vow
        Love's joy t' impart !
    Assay the while
    How to beguile :
        Farewell, faint heart.
Taken she is, new joys I must approve ;
Phyllis doth sleep and I will kiss my love.

Now peep, bo-peep ; be not too bold, my hand :
Wake not thy Phillis, fear she do withstand.
    She stirs alas,
    Alas, alas !
        I faint in sprite :

---

[1] Old ed. "hers."

                She opes her eye,
                Unhappy I !
                    Farewell, delight !
            Awaked she is, new woes I must approve,
            Phillis awakes and I must leave my love.

                            From THOMAS CAMPION'S
                                Fourth Book of Airs (circ.
                                1617).

O LOVE, where are thy shafts, thy quiver, and thy
        bow ?
Shall my wounds only weep and he ungaged go ?
Be just and strike him too that dares contemn thee so.

No eyes are like to thine, though men suppose thee
        blind,
So fair they level when the mark they list to find ;
Then strike, O strike the heart that bears the cruel
        mind.

Is my fond sight deceived, or do I Cupid spy
Close aiming at his breast by whom despised I die ?
Shoot home, sweet Love, and wound him that he may
        not fly ?

O then we both will sit in some unhaunted shade
And heal each other's wound which Love hath justly
        made :
O hope, O thought too vain, how quickly dost thou
        fade !

At large he wanders still, his heart is free from pain,
While secret sighs I spend and tears, but all in vain :
Yet, Love, thou knowest, by right I should not thus
    complain.

From ROBERT JONES' *First Book of Airs*, 1601.

O MY poor eyes, the sun whose shine
Late gave you light, doth now decline
    And, set to you, to others riseth.
She, who would sooner die than change,
Not fearing death, delights to range,
    And now, O now, my soul despiseth.

Yet, O my heart, thy state is blest
To seek out rest in thy unrest,
    Since thou her slave no more remainest;
For she that bound thee sets thee free
Then when she first forsaketh thee :
    Such, O such, right by wrong thou gainest.

Eyes, gaze no more ! heart, learn to hate !
Experience tells you all too late
    Fond woman's love with faith still warreth :
While true desert speaks, writes and gives,
Some groom the bargain nearer drives
    And he, O he, the market marreth.

From Martin Peerson's *Private Music*, 1620.

O PRECIOUS time, created by the might
    Of His blest word that made all comely features,
And wisely parted into day and night
For the best use and service of the [1] creatures :
O woe is me that have misspent this treasure
In vain delight of fond and wicked pleasure !

From John Coperario's *Funeral Tears*, 1606.

O SWEET flower, too quickly fading,
    Like a winter sunshine day !
    Poor pilgrim tired in the mid-way !
Like the earth, itself half shading,
So thy picture shows to me
But only the one half of thee.

O dear joy, too swiftly flying
    From thy love's enchanted eyes !
    Proud glory spread through the vast skies,
Earth of more than earth envying :
O how wondrous hadst thou been
Had but the world thy whole life seen !

[1] Qy. " His " ?

From JOHN DOWLAND'S *Third
Book of Songs or Airs*, 1603.

O WHAT hath overwrought
   My all-amazed thought?
Or whereto am I brought,
That thus in vain have sought,
Till time and truth hath taught
I labour all for nought?

The day, I see, is clear,
But I am ne'er the near;[1]
For grief doth still appear
To cross our merry cheer,
While I can nothing here
But winter all the year.

Cold, hold! the sun will shine warm:
Therefore now fear no harm.
O·blessed beams, where beauty streams,
Happy, happy light, to love's dreams!

[1] "Ne'er the near,"—never the nearer.

From *Gesta Graiorum : Gray's Inn Masque*, 1594. (By THOMAS CAMPION.)

A HYMN IN PRAISE OF NEPTUNE.

OF Neptune's empire let us sing,
  At whose command the waves obey;
To whom the rivers tribute pay,
Down the high mountains sliding':
To whom the scaly nation yields
Homage for the crystal fields
    Wherein they dwell :
And every sea-god pays a gem
Yearly out of his wat'ry cell
To deck great Neptune's diadem.

The Tritons dancing in a ring,
Before his palace-gates do make
The water with their echoes quake,
Like the great thunder sounding:
The sea-nymphs chaunt their accents shrill,
And the sirens, taught to kill
    With their sweet voice,
Make ev'ry echoing rock reply,
Unto their gentle murmuring noise,
The praise of Neptune's empery.

From Thomas Morley's
Madrigals to Four Voices,
1600.

ON a fair morning, as I came by the way,
   Met I with a merry maid in the merry month of
     May,
When a sweet love sings his lovely lay
And every bird upon the bush bechirps it up so gay,
With a heave and ho ! with a heave and ho !
Thy wife shall be thy master, I trow.
Sing, care away, care away, let the world go !
Hey, lustily all in a row, all in a row,
Sing, care away, care away, let the world go !

From Robert Jones' *The Muses'
Garden of Delights*, 1610.

ONCE did my thoughts both ebb and flow,
   As passion did them move ;
Once did I hope, straight fear again,—
   And then I was in love.

Once did I waking spend the night,
   And tell how many minutes move.
Once did I wishing waste the day,—
   And then I was in love.

Once, by my carving true love's knot,
   The weeping trees did prove
That wounds and tears were both our lot,—
   And then I was in love.

Once did I breathe another's breath
   And in my mistress move,
Once was I not mine own at all,—
   And then I was in love.

Once wore I bracelets made of hair,
   And collars did approve,
Once wore my clothes made out of wax,—
   And then I was in love.

Once did I sonnet to my saint,
   My soul in numbers move,
Once did I tell a thousand lies,—
   And then I was in love.

Once in my ear did dangling hang
   A little turtle-dove,
Once, in a word, I was a fool,—
   And then I was in love.

From THOMAS BATESON'S *Second
Set of Madrigals*, 1618.

ONE woman scarce of twenty
   But hath of tears great plenty,
Which they pour out like fountains
That run down from the mountains:

Yet all is but beguiling,
Their tears and eke their smiling.
I'll therefore never trust them,
Since nature hath so cursed them
That they can weep in smiling,
Poor fools thereby beguiling.

From MARTIN PEERSON'S *Private Music*, 1620.

"OPEN the door! Who's there within?
　The fairest of thy mother's kin,
O come, come, come abroad
And hear the shrill birds sing,
　The air with tunes that load!
It is too soon to go to rest,
The sun not midway yet to west:
　The day doth miss thee
And will not part until it kiss thee."

"Were I as fair as you pretend,
Yet to an unknown seld-seen[1] friend
I dare not ope the door:
　To hear the sweet birds sing
　Oft proves a dangerous thing.
The sun may run his wonted race
And yet not gaze on my poor face,
　The day may miss me:
Therefore depart, you shall not kiss me."

[1] *i.e.*, seldom seen.

From ROBERT JONES' *First Book
of Songs and Airs*, 1601.

PERPLEXED sore am I:
    Thine eyes' fair love, like Phœbus' brightest
  beams,
  Doth set my heart on fire and daze my sight;
  Yet do I live by virtue of those beams,
  For when thy face is hid comes fearful night.
Then since my eyes cannot endure so heavenly spark,
Sweet, grant that I may still feel out my love by dark.

    So shall I joyful be:
  Each thing on earth that liveth by the sun
  Would die if he in glory still appear:
  Then let some clouds of pity overrun
  That glorious face, that I with lively cheer
    May stand up before thee;
Or, since my eyes cannot endure so heavenly spark,
Sweet, grant that I may still feel out my love by dark.

From Add. MS., 18936.

PHILLIS, a herd-maid dainty,
  Who hath no peer for beauty,
By Thyrsis was requested
To hear the wrongs wherewith his heart was wrested;
But she Diana served
And would not hear how Love poor lovers sterved.

Phillis, more white than lilies,
More fair than Amaryllis,
More cold than crystal fountain,
More hard than craggy rock or stony mountain,
O tiger fierce and spiteful,
Why hate'st thou Love sith Love is so delightful?

From CAMPION *and* ROSSETER'S
Book of Airs, 1601.

REPROVE not love, though fondly thou hast lost
   Greater hopes by loving:
Love calms ambitious spirits, from their breast
   Dangers oft removing.
Let lofty humours mount up on high,
   Down again like to the wind;
While private thoughts bowed to love,
   More peace and pleasure find.

Love and sweet beauty makes the stubborn mild,
   And the coward fearless;
The wretched miser's care to bounty turns;
   Cheering all things cheerless.
Love chains the earth and heaven,
   Turns the spheres, guides the years in endless peace:
The flowery earth through his power
   Receives her due increase.

From THOMAS CAMPION'S *Fourth
Book of Airs* (circ. 1617).

RESPECT my faith, regard my service past,
The hope you winged call home to you at last;
Great price it is that I in you shall gain,
So great for you hath been my loss and pain:
My wits I spent and time for you alone,
Observing you and losing all for one.

Some raised to rich estates in this time are
That held their hopes to mine inferior far;
Such, scoffing me or pitying me, say thus,
" Had he not loved he might have lived like us."
O then, dear sweet, for love and pity's sake,
My love reward and from me scandal take.

From JOHN DOWLAND'S *First
Book of Songs or Airs*, 1597.

REST awhile, you cruel cares,
Be not more severe than love;
Beauty kills and beauty spares,
And sweet smiles sad sighs remove.
Laura, fair queen of my delight,
Come, grant me love in love's despite;
And if I ever fail to honour thee,
    Let this heavenly light I see
    Be as dark as hell to me!

If I speak, my words want weight;
Am I mute, my heart doth break;
If I sigh, she fears deceit;
Sorrow then for me must speak.
Cruel, unkind, with favour view
The wound that first was made by you!
And if my torments feigned be,
    Let this heavenly light I see
    Be as dark as hell to me.

Never hour of pleasing rest
Shall revive my dying ghost
Till my soul hath repossest
The sweet hope which love hath lost.
Laura, redeem the soul that dies
By fury of thy murdering eyes;
And if it proves unkind to thee
    Let this heavenly light I see
    Be as dark as hell to me.

From Add. MS. 15, 117.

A DIALOGUE.

1. SAY, fond Love, what seeks thou here
    In the silence of the night?
2. Here I seek those joys, my dear,
    That in silence[1] most delight.
1. Night's heavy humour calls to sleep.
2.   But love's humour watch doth keep:
    Let never humour happy prove
    But that which only pleaseth love.

[1] MS. "silent."

From JOHN DOWLAND'S *Third Book of Songs or Airs*, 1603.

"Say, Love, if ever thou didst find
   A woman with a constant mind."
          "None but one."
"And what should that rare mirror be?"
"Some goddess or some queen is She."
She, She, She, and only She,
She only queen of love and beauty.

"But could thy fiery poisoned dart
At no time touch her spotless heart,
        Nor come near?"
"She is not subject to Love's bow:
Her eye commands, her heart saith 'No.'"
No, no, no, and only No,
One No another still doth follow.

"How might I that fair wonder know
That mocks desire with endless 'No?'"
       "See the moon
That ever in one change doth grow,
Yet still the same : and She is so."
So, so, so, and only So!
From heaven her virtues she doth borrow.

"To her then yield thy shafts and bow
That can command affections so."
        "Love is free :

So are her thoughts that vanquish thee.
There is no queen of love but She."
She, She, She, and only She,
She only queen of love and beauty.

> From CAMPION and ROSSETER'S
> *Book of Airs*, 1601.

SEE where she flies enraged from me !
 View her when she intends despite,
The wind is not more swift than she.
Her fury moved such terror makes
As to a fearful guilty sprite
The voice of heaven's huge thunder-cracks :
But when her appeased mind yields to delight,
All her thoughts are made of joys,
Millions of delights inventing ;
Other pleasures are but toys
To her beauty's sweet contenting.

My fortune hangs upon her brow ;
For as she smiles or frowns on me,
So must my blown affections bow ;
And her proud thoughts too well do find
With what unequal tyranny
Her beauties do command my mind.
Though, when her sad planet reigns,
Froward she be,
She alone can pleasure move
And displeasing sorrow banish.
May I but still hold her love,
Let all other comforts vanish.

From FRANCIS PILKINGTON'S
First Set of Madrigals, 1614.

SEE where my love a-maying goes,
    With sweet dame Flora sporting!
She most alone with nightingales
    In woods delights consorting.
Turn again, my dearest!
    The pleasant'st air's in meadows:
Else by the rivers let us breathe,
    And kiss amongst the willows.

From WILLIAM CORKINE'S
Second Book of Airs, 1612.

SHALL a smile or guileful glance,
    Or a sigh that is but feigned,
Shall but tears that come by chance
    Make me dote that was disdained?
    No; I will no more be chained.

Shall I sell my freedom so,
    Being now from Love remised?
Shall I learn (what I do know
    To my cost) that Love's disguised?
    No; I will be more advised.

Must she fall, and I must stand?
    Must she fly, and I pursue her?
Must I give her heart and land,
    And, for nought, with them endue her?
    No; first I will find her truer.

From WILLIAM CORKINE'S
Second Book of Airs, 1612.

SHALL I be with toys[1] deceived?
  Can Love's bands be sealed with kisses?
Cupid, of his eyes bereaved,
  Yet in darkness seldom misses:
  Let not dallying lose these blisses.

Sleep hath sealed their eyes and ears
  That our loves so long have guarded:
Hymen hides your maiden fears,
  Now my love may be rewarded:
  Let my suit be now regarded.

From ROBERT JONES' *Ultimum Vale*, 1608.

SINCE just[2] disdain began to rise
  And cry revenge for spiteful wrong,
What erst I prayed I now despise
And think my love was too-too long;
I tread in dirt that scornful pride
Which in thy looks I have descried;
Thy beauty is a painted skin
For fools to see their faces in.

---

[1] Old ed. "joyes."
[2] "Just" is the reading in Davison's *Poetical Rhapsody*, 1602, and Martin Peerson's *Private Music*, 1620.—Jones gives "first."

Thine eyes, that some as stars esteem
From whence themselves, they say, take light,
Like to the foolish fire I deem
That leads men to their death by night ;
Thy words and oaths are light as wind,
And yet far lighter is thy mind ;
Thy friendship is a broken reed
That fails thy friend in greatest need.

From ROBERT JONES' *First Set of Madrigals*, 1607.

SING, merry birds, your cheerful notes !
   For Progne you have seen
To come from Summer's Queen.
O tune, O tune your throats !
Forgetting all cold Winter's harm,
Now may we perch on branches green,
And singing sit and not be seen.

From THOMAS MORLEY'S *Plain and Easy Introduction to Practical Music*, 1597.

SLEEP, O sleep, fond fancy,
   My head, alas, thou tirest
With false delight of that which thou desirest.
Sleep, I say, fond fancy,
And leave my thoughts molesting :
Thy master's head hath need of sleep and resting.

From MICHAEL ESTE'S *Madrigals*, 1604.

SLY thief, if so you will believe,
  It nought or little did me grieve,
That my true heart you had bereft,
Till that unkindly you it left :
Leaving you lose, losing you kill
That which I may forego so ill.

What thing more cruel can you do
Than rob a man and kill him too?
Wherefore of love I ask this meed,
To bring you where you did this deed,
That there you may, for your amisses [1]
Be damaged in a thousand kisses.

From THOMAS CAMPION'S *Third Book of Airs* (circ. 1617).

SO quick, so hot, so mad is thy fond suit,
  So rude, so tedious grown in urging me,
That fain I would with loss make thy tongue mute,
  And yield some little grace to quiet thee :
An hour with thee I care not to converse,
For I would not be counted too perverse.

But roofs too hot would prove for me [2] all fire,
  And hills too high for my unused pace ;
The grove is charged with thorns and the bold briar,
  Grey snakes the meadows shroud in every place :
A yellow frog, alas ! will fright me so
As I should start and tremble as I go.

[1] Faults.   [2] Old ed. "men"

Since then I can on earth no fit room find,
    In heaven I am resolved with you to meet :
Till then, for hope's sweet sake, rest your tired mind,
    And not so much as see me in the street :
A heavenly meeting one day we shall have,
But never, as you dream, in bed or grave.

> From *Musica Transalpina.* *The Second Book of Madrigals,* 1597.

SO saith my fair and beautiful Lycoris,
    When now and then she talketh
With me of love :
" Love is a sprite that walketh,
That soars and flies,
And none alive can hold him,
Nor touch him, nor behold him."
Yet when her eye she turneth,
I spy where he sojourneth :
In her eyes there he flies,
But none can catch him
Till from her lips he fetch him.

> From THOMAS CAMPION'S *Fourth Book of Airs* (circ. 1617).

SO sweet is thy discourse to me,
    And so delightful is thy sight,
As I taste nothing right but thee :
    O why invented Nature light ?
Was it alone for Beauty's sake
That her graced words might better take ?

No more can I old joys recall,
   They now to me become unknown,
Not seeming to have been at all :
   Alas, how soon is this love grown
To such a spreading height in me
As with it all must shadowed be !

From ROBERT JONES' *The Muses'*
Garden of Delights, 1610.

SOFT, Cupid, soft, there is no haste,
   For all unkindness gone and past ;
Since thou wilt needs forsake me so,
Let us part friends before thou go.

Still shalt thou have my heart to use,—
When[1] I cannot otherwise chuse :
My life thou mayst command sans doubt,
Command, I say,—and go without.

And if that I do ever prove
False and unkind to gentle Love,
I'll not desire to live a day
Nor any longer—than I may.

I'll daily bless the little god,—
But not without a smarting rod.
Wilt thou still unkindly leave me?
Now I pray God,—all ill go with thee !

[1] Qy. "When otherwise I cannot chuse"?

> From GILES FARNABY'S *Canzonets*, 1598.

SOMETIME she would and sometime not,
　　The more request the more disdain'd;
Each woman hath her gift, God wot,
　And ever had since Venus reign'd :
Though Vulcan did to Venus yield,
I would have men to win the field.

> From JOHN WILBYE'S *Second Set of Madrigals*, 1609.

STAY, Corydon, thou swain,
　　Talk not so soon of dying;
What, though thy heart be slain,
　What, if thy love be flying?
She threatens thee, but dare not strike;
Thy nymph is light and shadow-like,
For if thou follow her she'll fly from thee,
But if thou fly from her she'll follow thee.

> From THOMAS BATESON'S *First Set of English Madrigals*, 1604.

SWEET Gemma, when I first beheld thy beauty,
　I vowed thee service, honour, love and duty :
O then, I said, the best
Is hither come to make me blest ;

But thou, alas! sweet, thou
Dost not regard my vow :
Go, go, let me not see
Cruel, though fairest, thee.

Yet stay! alway be chained to my heart
With links of love that we do never part!
Then I'll not call thee serpent, tiger, cruel,
But my sweet Gemma and my fairest jewel.

From ROBERT JONES' *Ultimum
Vale*, 1608.

SWEET, if you like and love me still
And yield me love for my good will,
And do not from your promise start
When your fair hand gave me your heart ;
 If dear to you I be
 As you are dear to me,
Then yours I am and will be ever :
Nor[1] time nor place my love shall sever,
But faithful still I will persever,
 Like constant marble stone,
 Loving but you alone.

But if you favour moe than one
(Who loves thee still and none but thee),

---

[1] This is the reading in Davison's *Poetical Rapsody*, where this song is printed with the heading "His farewell to his unkind and inconstant mistress."—The songbook gives "No time nor place".

If others do the harvest gain
That's due to me for all my pain;
   If[1] that you love to range
   And oft to chop and change,
Then get you some new-fangled mate;
My doting love shall turn to hate,
Esteeming you (though too-too late)
   Not worth a pebble stone,
   Loving not me alone.[2]

From WILLIAM CORKINE'S
Airs, 1610.

SWEET, let me go! sweet, let me go!
  What do you mean to vex me so?
Cease your pleading force!
Do you think thus to extort remorse?
Now, now! no more! alas, you overbear me,
And I would cry,—but some would hear, I fear me.

From THOMAS BATESON'S *Second
Set of Madrigals*, 1618.

SWEET, those trammels of your hair
  Golden locks more truly are,
My thoughts locking to thy beauty.
Thus you do my captive mind

---

[1] Old ed., "Yet."
[2] So Davison.—In the songbook the line stands "Loving me not alone."

From my dying body bind,
Only to you to do duty.

Oh, my dear, let it go free,
Or my body take to thee!
So your captive you shall cherish ;
For if parted thus they lie,
Or my thoughts or I must die :
'Twill grieve thee if either perish.

From *Christ Church MS.* K. 3.
43-5.

SWEET, yet cruel unkind is she
To creep into my heart and murder me.
Yet those beams from her eyes
Dims Apollo at his rise ;
And all these purer graces,
All in their several places,
Begets a glory doth surprise
All hearts, all eyes,
For only she
Gives life eternity ;
And when her presence deigns but to appear
Never wish greater bliss than shines from her bright
    sphere :
Her absence wounds, strikes dead all hearts with fear.

From ALFONSO FERRABOSCO'S
Airs, 1609.

A Dialogue between a Shepherd and a Nymph.

1 TELL me, O Love, when shall it be
   That thy fair eyes shall shine on me,
     Whom nothing else reviveth?
2 I pray thee, shepherd, leave thy fears,
   Drown not thy heart and eyes with tears;
     Such sighs my sense depriveth.

1 Alas, sweet nymph! I cannot chuse,
   Since thou estranged lives from me.
2 O do not me for that accuse;
   My love, my life, doth live in thee.
1 Alas what joy is in such love
     That ever lives apart,
   And never other comforts prove
     But cares that kill the heart!
   O let me die!

2 And so will I.
   Yet stay, sweet Love, and sing this song with me:
   'Time brings to pass what love thinks could not be.'

From CAMPION and ROSSETER'S
Book of Airs, 1601.

THE cypress curtain of the night is spread,
    And over all a silent dew is cast;
The weaker cares by sleep are conquered,
    But I alone, with hideous grief aghast,

In spite of Morpheus' charms a watch do keep
Over mine eyes, to banish careless sleep.

Yet oft my trembling eyes through faintness close,
    And then the Map of Hell before me stands,
Which ghosts do see, and I am one of those
    Ordained to pine in sorrow's endless bands ;
Since from my wretched soul all hopes are reft,
And now no cause of life to me is left.

Grief, seize my soul ! for that will still endure
    When my crazed body is consumed and gone :
Bear it to thy black den, there keep it sure,
    Where thou ten thousand souls dost tire upon :
Yet all do not afford such food to thee
As this poor one, the worser part of me.

                  From WILLIAM BYRD'S *Psalms*
                      Songs, and Sonnets, 1611.

THE eagle's force subdues each bird that flies ;
    What metal may resist the flaming fire ?
Doth not the sun dazzle the clearest eyes,
    And melt the ice, and make the frost retire ?
    Who can withstand a puissant king's desire ?
The stiffest stones are pierced through with tools :
The wisest are with Princes made but fools.

From ROBERT JONES' *The Muses'
Garden of Delights*, 1610.

THE fountains smoke, and yet no flames they show ;
　　Stars shine by night, though undiscerned by day;
And trees do spring, yet are not seen to grow ;
And shadows move, although they seem to stay :
In Winter's woe is buried Summer's bliss,
And Love loves most when love most secret is.

The stillest streams descry the greatest deep ;
The clearest sky is subject to a shower ;
Conceit's most sweet whenas it seems to sleep,
And fairest days do in the morning lower :
The silent groves sweet nymphs they cannot miss,
For Love loves most where love most secret is.

The rarest jewels hidden virtue yield ;
The sweet of traffic is a secret gain ;
The year once old doth show a barren field ;
And plants seem dead, and yet they spring again :
Cupid is blind, the reason why is this,
Love loveth most when love most secret is.

From JOHN ATTEY'S *First Book
of Airs*, 1622.

THE Gordian knot, which Alexander great
　　Did whilom cut with his all-conquering sword,
Was nothing like thy busk-point, pretty peat,[1]
　Nor could so fair an augury afford,
Which if I chance to cut or else untie,
Thy little world I'll conquer presently.

[1] Pet.

From *Christ Church MS.*, *K.* 3, 47. (Music by THOMAS WEELKES.)

THE greedy wretch that surfeits on his gold
   And multiplies his store by usury,
Ne'er thinks on death or that he shall grow old,
Till death approach : Oh, then he fears to die,
And when he hears the knowling [*sic*] of the bell
With coward heart he bids the world farewell.

From THOMAS BATESON'S *Second Set of Madrigals*, 1618.

THE nightingale in silent night
   Doth sing as well as in the light ;
To lull Love's watchful eyes asleep
She doth such nightly sonnets keep.
Heigh ho ! sing we withal,
What fortune us soe'er befall.

From JOHN BARTLET'S *Airs*, 1606.

THE Queen of Paphos, Erycine,
   In heart did rose-cheek'd Adon love
He mortal was, but she divine,
   And oft with kisses did him move ;
With great gifts still she did him woo,
But he would never yield thereto.

Then since the Queen of Love by Love
  To love was once a subject made,
And could thereof no pleasure prove,
  By day, by night, by light or shade,
Why, being mortal, should I grieve,
Since she herself could not relieve?

She was a goddess heavenly
  And loved a fair-faced earthly boy,
Who did contemn her deity
  And would not grant her hope of joy;
For Love doth govern by a fate
That here plants will and there leaves hate.

But I a hapless mortal wight
  To an immortal beauty sue;
No marvel then she loathes my sight
  Since Adon Venus would not woo.
Hence groaning sighs, mirth be my friend!
Before my life, my love shall end.

From Robert Jones' The
Muses' Garden of Delights,
1610.

THE sea hath many thousand sands,
  The sun hath motes as many;
The sky is full of stars, and love
  As full of woes as any:
Believe me, that do know the elf,
And make no trial by thyself.

It is in truth a pretty toy
For babes to play withal;
But O the honies of our youth
Are oft our age's gall!
Self-proof in time will make thee know
He was a prophet told thee so:

A prophet that, Cassandra-like,
Tells truth without belief;
For headstrong youth will run his race,
Although his goal be grief:
Love's martyr, when his heat is past,
Proves Care's confessor at the last.

From MARTIN PEERSON'S *Private Music*, 1620.

THE spring of joy is dry
   That ran into my heart,
And all my comforts fly:
   My love and I must part.

Farewell, my love, I go,
If Fate will have it so!
Yet, to content us both,
Return again as doth
    The bee unto the flower,
        The cattle to the brook,
    The shadow to the hour,
        The fish unto the hook,
That we may sport our fill
And love continue still.

From RICHARD CARLTON'S
Madrigals, 1601.

THE witless boy that blind is to behold,
  Yet blinded sees what in our fancy lies,
With smiling looks and hairs of curled gold
  Hath oft entrapped and oft deceived the wise :
No wit can serve his fancy to remove,
For finest wits are soonest thralled to Love.

From THOMAS CAMPION'S *Two
Books of Airs* (circ. 1613).

THERE is none, O none but you,
  That from me estrange your sight,
Whom mine eyes affect to view
  Or chained ears hear with delight.

Other beauties others move,
  In you I all graces find ;
Such is the effect of Love,
  To make them happy that are kind.

Women in frail beauty trust,
  Only seem you fair to me ;
Yet prove truly kind and just,
  For that may not dissembled be.

Sweet, afford me then your sight,
  That, surveying all your looks,
Endless volumes I may write
  And fill the world with envied books:

Which when after-ages view,
  All shall wonder and despair,
Woman to find man so true,
  Or man a woman half so fair.

From Christ Church MS. I. 5. 49.
(Music by ALFONSO FERRA-
BOSCO.)

THERE was a frog swum in the lake,
  The crab came crawling by:
"Wilt thou," coth the frog, "be my make [1]?"
Coth the crab "No, not I."
"My skin is s[m]ooth and dappled fine,
I can leap far and nigh.
Thy shell is hard: so is not mine."
Coth the crab "No, not I."
"Tell me," then spake the crab, "therefore,
Or else I thee defy:
Give me thy claw, I ask no more."
Coth the frog "That will I."
The crab bit off the frog's fore-feet;
The frog then he must die.
To woo a crab it is not meet:
If any do, it is not I.

[1] The MS. gives "mate"; but I read "make" (an old form of "mate") for the sake of the rhyme.

From ROBERT JONES' *First Set
of Madrigals*, 1607.

THINE eyes so bright
  Bereft my sight
    When first I view'd thy face;
So now my light
Is turn'd to night,
  I stray from place to place:
Then guide me of thy kindness,
So shall I bless my blindness.

From WILLIAM BARLEY'S *New
Book of Tabliture*, 1596.

THOSE eyes that set my fancy on a fire,
  Those crisped hairs that hold my heart in chains,
Those dainty hands which conquered my desire,
  That wit which of my thoughts doth hold the reins:
Then Love be judge, what heart may therewith stand
Such eyes, such head, such wit, and such a hand?
Those eyes for clearness doth the stars surpass,
  Those hairs obscure the brightness of the sun,
Those hands more white than ever ivory was,
  That wit even to the skies hath glory won.
O eyes that pierce our hearts without remorse!
  O hairs of right that wear a royal crown!
O hands that conquer more than Cæsar's force!
  O wit that turns huge kingdoms upside down!

From Thomas Weelkes'
Madrigals, 1597.

THOSE spots upon my lady's face appearing,
    The one of black, the other bright carnation,
Are like the mulberries in dainty gardens growing,
    Where grows delight and pleasures of rich fashion:
They grow too high and warily kept from me,
Which makes me sing "Ay me! 'twill never be."

From Thomas Campion's *Fourth
Book of Airs* (circ. 1617).

THOU joyest, fond boy, to be by many loved,
    To have thy beauty of most dames approved;
For this dost thou thy native worth disguise
And playest the sycophant t'observe their eyes:
Thy glass thou counsell'st, more to adorn thy skin,
That first should school thee to be fair within.

'Tis childish to be caught with pearl or amber,
And womanlike too much to cloy the chamber;
Youths should the fields affect, heat their rough steeds,
Their hardened nerves to fit for better deeds:
Is't not more joy strongholds to force with swords
Than women's weakness take with looks or words?

Men that do noble things all purchase glory,
One man for one brave act hath proved a story;
But if that one ten thousand dames o'ercame,
Who would record it, if not to his shame?
'Tis far more conquest with one to live true
Than every hour to triumph lord of new.

From Mus. Sch. MS. F. 575.

THOU sent'st to me a heart was crowned;
    I took it to be thine,
But when I saw it had a wound
    I knew that heart was mine.
A bounty of a strange conceit!
    To send mine own to me,
And send it in a worse estate
    Than when it came to thee.

From JOHN HILTON's Airs, 1627.

THOUGH me you disdain to view,
    Yet give me leave to gaze on you:
The sun as yet did never hide him
When a Moor or Tartar eyed him.
        Fa la la!

From CAMPION and ROSSETER'S
Book of Airs, 1601.

THOUGH you are young and I am old,
  Though your veins hot and my blood cold;
Though youth is moist and age is dry,
Yet embers live when flames do die.

The tender graft is easily broke,
But who shall shake the sturdy oak?
You are more fresh and fair than I;
Yet stubs do live when flowers do die.

Thou, that thy youth dost vainly boast,
Know buds are soonest nipped with frost;
Think that thy fortune still doth cry,
"Thou fool! tomorrow thou must die."

From THOMAS WEELKES'
Madrigals of Five and Six Parts, 1600.

THREE times a day my prayer is
  To gaze my fill on Thoralis,
And three times thrice I daily pray
Not to offend that sacred may [1];
But all the year my suit must be
That I may please and she love me.

[1] Maid.

From THOMAS WEELKES'
Madrigals of Six Parts,
1600.

THULE, the period of cosmography,
    Doth vaunt of Hecla, whose sulphureous fire
Doth melt the frozen clime and thaw the sky,
    Trinacrian Aetna's flames ascend not higher:
These things seem wondrous, yet more wondrous I,
Whose heart with fear doth freeze, with love doth fry.

The Andalusian merchant, that returns
    Laden with cochineal and china dishes,
Reports in Spain how strangely Fogo burns
    Amidst an ocean full of flying fishes:
These things seem wondrous, yet more wondrous I,
Whose heart with fear doth freeze, with love doth fry.

From THOMAS MORLEY'S *The
First Book of Airs,* 1600.

THYRSIS and Milla, arm in arm together,
    In merry may-time to the green garden walked,
Where all the way they wanton riddles talked;
The youthful boy, kissing her cheeks so rosy,
Beseech'd her there to gather him a posy.

She straight her light green silken coats uptucked
And may for Mill and thyme for Thyrsis plucked;
Which when she brought, he clasp'd her by the middle
And kiss'd her sweet, but could not read her riddle.
"Ah fool!" with that the nymph set up a laughter,
And blush'd, and ran away, and he ran after.

From JOHN DANYEL'S *Songs for the Lute, Viol, and Voice,* 1606.

TIME, cruel Time, canst thou subdue that brow
   That conquers all but thee, and thee too stays,
As if she were exempt from scythe or bow,
   From Love and Years, unsubject to decays?

Or art thou grown in league with those fair eyes
   That they might help thee to consume our days?
Or dost thou love her for her cruelties,
   Being merciless like thee, that no man weighs?

Then do so still, although she makes no 'steem
   Of days nor years, but lets them run in vain:
Hold still thy swift-wing'd hours, that wond'ring seem
   To gaze on her, even to turn back again.

And do so still, although she nothing cares:
   Do as I do, love her although unkind:
Hold still, yet O! I fear at unawares
   Thou wilt beguile her though thou seem'st so kind.

> From JOHN DOWLAND'S *Second
> Book of Songs or Airs*, 1600.

TIME'S eldest son, Old Age (the heir of Ease,
  Strength's foe, Love's woe, and foster to Devotion)
Bids gallant Youth in martial prowess please ;
As for himself, he hath no earthly motion,
But thinks sighs, tears, vows, prayers and sacrifices,
As good as shows, masques, jousts or tilt-devices.

Then sit thee down and say thy *Nunc dimittis*,
With *De Profundis*, *Credo*, and *Te Deum* ;
Chant *Miserere*, for what now so fit is
As that or this, *Paratum est cor meum?*
O that thy saint would take in worth thy heart !
Thou canst not please her with a better part.

When others sing *Venite exultemus*,
Stand by and turn to *Nolo æmulari* ;
For *Quare fremuerunt* use *Oremus* ;
Vivat Eliza for an *Ave Mary* !
And teach those swains that lives about thy cell
To sing *Amen* when thou dost pray so well.

From MICHAEL ESTE'S *Madrigals*, 1604.

"TO bed, to bed!" she calls and never ceaseth:
　　Which words do pierce and grieve my heart
full sore.
"To bed, to bed!" I say, my pain increaseth;
　Yet I'll to bed and trouble you no more.
Good night, sweet heart! to bed I must begone,
And being there I'll muse on thee alone.

From THOMAS WEELKES' *Airs or Fantastic Spirits*, 1608.

TO-MORROW is the marriage-day
　Of Mopsus and fair Phyllida:
Come, shepherds, bring your garlands gay.

If Love lie in so foul a nest,
And foulness on so fair a breast,
What lover may not hope the best?

O do not weep, fair Bellamour:
Though he be gone, there's many more,
For Love hath many loves in store.

> From THOMAS CAMPION'S *Two
> Books of Airs* (circ. 1613.)

TO music bent is my retired mind
   And fain would I some song of pleasure sing,
But in vain joys no comfort now I find,
From heavenly thoughts all true delight doth spring :
Thy power, O God, Thy mercies to record,
Will sweeten every note and every word.

All earthly pomp or beauty to express
Is but to carve in snow, on waves to write ;
Celestial things, though men conceive them less,
Yet fullest are they in themselves of light :
Such beams they yield as know no means to die,
Such heat they cast as lifts the spirit high.

> From ORLANDO GIBBONS' *First
> Set of Madrigals*, 1612.

TRUST not too much, fair youth, unto thy feature,
   Be not enamoured of thy blushing hue ;
Be gamesome whilst thou art a goodly creature ;
   The flowers will fade that in thy garden grew :
Sweet violets are gather'd in their spring,
White primit [1] falls withouten pitying.

[1] Privet.

From WILLIAM CORKINE'S
Second Book of Airs, 1612.

TRUTH-TRYING Time shall cause my mistress say
My love was perfect, constant as the day:
And as the day when evening doth appear
Doth suffer doom to be or foul or clear,
So shall my last bequest make known to all
My love in her did rise, did live, did fall.

You Gods of Love, who oft heard my desires,
Prepare her heart by your love-charming fires
To think on those sweet revels, peaceful fights,
Ne'er-changing Custom taught at nuptial rites:
O guerdonize my prayers but with this,
That I may taste of that long-wished-for bliss.

From CAMPION and ROSSETER'S
Book of Airs, 1601.

TURN back, you wanton flyer,
    And answer my desire
  With mutual greeting.
Yet bend a little nearer,
True beauty still shines clearer
  In closer meeting.

Hearts with hearts delighted
Should strive to be united,
   Each other's arms with arms enchaining :
Hearts with a thought,
   Rosy lips with a kiss still entertaining.

What harvest half so sweet is
As still to reap the kisses
   Grown ripe in sowing?
And straight to be receiver
Of that which thou art giver,
   Rich in bestowing?
There is no strict observing
Of times' or seasons' swerving,[1]
   There is ever one fresh spring abiding :
Then what we sow with our lips,
   Let us reap, love's gains dividing.

From *Christ Church MS. I.* 4. 78.

TURN in, my Lord, turn into me,
   My heart's a homely place ;
But thou canst make corruption flee
And fill it with thy grace :
So furnished it will be brave,
And a rich dwelling thou shalt have.

[1] Old ed. "changing."

From THOMAS VAUTOR'S *Songs
of divers Airs and Natures,*
1619.

UNKIND, is this the meed of lovers' pain?
   Doth loyal faith no better guerdon gain?
Adieu! thy looks are coy, thy fancy strange:
O, stay! my heart relents and will not change,
But rather die than from my saint once swerve:
My life she gave, my love she doth deserve.

From JOHN DOWLAND'S *First
Book of Songs or Airs,* 1597.

UNQUIET thoughts, your civil slaughter stint,
   And wrap your wrongs within a pensive heart;
And you, my tongue, that makes my mouth a mint
And stamps my thoughts to coin them words by art,
Be still! for if you ever do the like,
I'll cut the string that makes the hammer strike.

But what can stay my thoughts they may not start?
Or put my tongue in durance for to die?
Whenas these eyes, the keys of mouth and heart,
Open the lock where all my love doth lie,
I'll seal them up within their lids for ever:
So thoughts and words and looks shall die together.

How shall I then gaze on my mistress' eyes?
My thoughts must have some vent, else heart will
    break.
My tongue would rust, as in my mouth it lies,
If eyes and thoughts were free and that not speak.
Speak then! and tell the passions of desire,
Which turns mine eyes to floods, my thoughts to fire.

From MARTIN PEERSON'S *Private Music*, 1620.

UPON my lap my sovereign sits
    And sucks upon my breast;
Meantime his love maintains my life
And gives my sense her rest.
    Sing lullaby, my little boy,
    Sing lullaby, mine only joy!

When thou hast taken thy repast,
Repose, my babe, on me;
So may thy mother and thy nurse
Thy cradle also be.
    Sing lullaby, my little boy,
    Sing lullaby, mine only joy!

I grieve that duty doth not work
All that my wishing would,
Because I would not be to thee
But in the best I should.
    Sing lullaby, my little boy,
    Sing lullaby, mine only joy!

Yet as I am, and as I may,
I must and will be thine,
Though all too little for thy self
Vouchsafing to be mine.
  Sing lullaby, my little boy,
  Sing lullaby, mine only joy!

From THOMAS CAMPION'S *Fourth Book of Airs* (circ. 1617).

VEIL, Love, mine eyes! O hide from me
   The plagues that charge the curious mind!
If beauty private will not be,
Suffice it yet that she proves kind.
Who can usurp heaven's light alone?
Stars were not made to shine on one.

Griefs past recure fools try to heal,
That greater harms on less inflict:
The pure offend by too much zeal,
Affection should not be too strict:
He that a true embrace will find
To beauty's faults must still be blind.

From *Christ Church MS. I.* 4. 78.

VICTORIOUS Time, whose winged feet do fly
   More swift than eagles in the azure sky,
Haste to thy prey, why art thou tardy now
When all things to thy powerful fate do bow?

O give an end to cares and killing fears,
Shake thy dull sand, unravel those few years
Are yet untold, since nought but discontents
Clouds all our earthly joy with sad laments,
That when thy nimble hours shall cease to be
We may be crown'd with blest eternity.

From THOMAS CAMPION'S *Two Books of Airs* (circ. 1613).

VIEW me, Lord, a work of Thine!
   Shall I then lie drown'd in night?
Might Thy grace in me but shine,
   I should seem made all of light.

But my soul still surfeits so
   On the poison'd baits of sin,
That I strange and ugly grow;
   All is dark and foul within.

Cleanse me, Lord, that I may kneel
   At thine altar pure and white:
They that once Thy mercies feel,
   Gaze no more on earth's delight.

Worldly joys like shadows fade
   When the heavenly light appears:
But the covenants Thou hast made,
   Endless, know nor days nor years.

In Thy Word, Lord, is my trust,
    To Thy mercies fast I fly;
Though I am but clay and dust,
    Yet Thy grace can lift me high.

From *Add. MS.* 17790.

WERE I made juror of that quest
    Where Venus' son should be arraign'd,
Before his fault were scarce exprest
    Or any party had complain'd,
I would cry "Guilty! the boy is guilty!"

And if by glancing of an eye
    A thief should slily steal a heart,
It should be counted felony;
    But if it did increase much smart,
I would cry "Murther! a grievous murther!"

But if another were repaid
    To satisfy for such a theft,
Though he had stol'n, it should be said
    He had as good behind him left,
And then cry "Quit him! O sweet thief! quit him!"

From JOHN DANYEL'S *Songs for
the Lute, Viol, and Voice,*
1606.

WHAT delight can they enjoy
    Whose hearts are not their own,
But are gone abroad astray
    And to others' bosoms flown?
Silly comforts, silly joy,
    Which fall and rise as others move
Who seldom use to turn our way!
    And therefore Chloris will not love,
        For well I see
        How false men be,
And let them pine that lovers prove.

From ROBERT JONES' *First Book of
Airs,* 1601.

WHAT if I seek for love of thee?
    Shall I find
    Beauty kind,
To desert that still shall dwell in me?
Though thy looks have charmed mine eyes,
I can forbear to love;
    But if ever sweet desire
    Set my woeful heart on fire,
Then can I never remove.

Frown not on me unless thou hate ;
    For thy frown
    Cast[s] me down
To despair of my most hapless state.
Smile not on me unless thou love ;
    For thy smile
    Will beguile
My desires, if thou unsteadfast prove.
If thou needs wilt bend thy brows,
A-while refrain, my dear ;
    But if thou wilt smile on me,
    Let it not delayed be :
Comfort is never too near.

From THOMAS CAMPION'S *Third
Book of Airs* (circ. 1617).

WHAT is it all that men possess, among themselves conversing ?
Wealth or fame or some such boast, scarce worthy the rehearsing.
Women only are men's good, with them in love conversing.

If weary, they prepare us rest ; if sick, their hand attends us ;
When with grief our hearts are prest, their comfort best befriends us ;
Sweet or sour, they willing go to share what fortune sends us.

What pretty babes with pain they bear, our name and
    form presenting!
What we get how wise they keep, by sparing wants
    preventing!
Sorting all their household cares to our observed con-
    tenting!

All this, of whose large use I sing, in two words is
    expressed:
GOOD WIFE is the good I praise, if by good men
    possessed.
Bad with bad in ill suit well, but good with good live
    blessed.

From THOMAS MORLEY'S *First
Book of Ballets to Five Voices*,
1600.

WHAT saith my dainty darling?
   Shall I now your love obtain?
Fa, la!
Long time I sued for grace,
  And grace you granted me
When time should serve and place:
  Can any fitter be?
Fa, la!

This crystal running fountain
  In his language saith "Come, Love!"
Fa, la!

  The birds, the trees, the fields,
   Else none can us behold ;
  This bank soft lying yields,
   And saith " Nice fools, be bold."
        Fa, la !

From Dr. John Wilson's *Cheerful Airs or Ballads*, 1660.

WHAT would any man desire ?
 Is he cold ? then, here's a fire.
Is he hot ? she'll gently school him
Till he find that heat does cool him.
Is he sad ? then here's a pleasure.
Is he poor ? then here's a treasure.
Loves he music ? here's the choice
Of all sweet sounds in her sweet voice.
Does he hunger ? here's a feast
To which a god might be a guest ;
And to those viands, if he thirst,
Here's nectar for him, since the first
Of men that was for sin a debtor
Never any tasted better.
Here's all complete from head to heel,
To hear, to see, taste, smell, or feel.

From JOHN BARTLET'S *Airs*,
1606.

WHEN from my love I look'd for love and kind
  affection's due,
Too well I found her vows to prove most faithless and
  untrue ;
For when I did ask her why,
Most sharply she did reply
That she with me did ne'er agree
To love but jestingly.

Mark but the subtle policies that female lovers find,
Who loves to fix their constancies like feathers in the
  wind ;
Though they swear, vow and protest
That they love you chiefly best,
Yet by-and-by they'll all deny,
And say 'twas but in jest.

From DR. JOHN WILSON'S *Cheerful Airs or Ballads*, 1660.

WHEN I behold my mistress' face
  Where beauty hath her dwelling-place,
And see those seeing stars her eyes
In whom love's fire for ever lies,
And hear her witty charming words
Her sweet tongue to mine ear affords,
Methinks he wants wit, ears, and eyes
Whom love makes not idolatrise.

From ROBERT JONES' *Musical
Dream*, 1609.

WHEN I sit reading all alone that secret book
    Wherein I sigh to look,
How many spots there be
I wish I could not see,
Or from myself might flee!

Mine eyes for refuge then with zeal befix the skies,
My tears do cloud those eyes,
My sighs do blow them dry;
And yet I live to die,
Myself I cannot fly.

Heavens, I implore, that knows my fault, what shall I
    do?
To Hell I dare not go;
The world first made me rue,
My self my griefs renew:
To whom then shall I sue?

Alas, my soul doth faint to draw this doubtful breath:
Is there no hope in death?
O yes, death ends my woes,
Death me from me will loose;
My self am all my foes.

From WILLIAM CORKINE'S
Second Book of Airs, 1612.

WHEN I was born Lucina cross-legged sate,
    The angry stars with ominous aspects
Frowned on my birth, and the foredooming Fate
    Ordained to brand me with their dire effects :
The sun did hide his face and left the night
To bring me to this world's accursed light.

From ROBERT JONES' *First Book
of Songs and Airs*, 1601.

WHEN love on time and measure makes his
    ground,
    Time that must end though love can never die,
'Tis love betwixt a shadow and a sound,
    A love not in the heart but in the eye ;
A love that ebbs and flows, now up, now down,
A morning's favour and an evening's frown.

Sweet looks show love, yet they are but as beams ;
    Fair words seem true, yet they are but as wind ;
Eyes shed their tears, yet are but outward streams ;
    Sighs paint a shadow in the falsest mind.
Looks, words, tears, sighs show love when love they
    leave ;
False hearts can weep, sigh, swear, and yet deceive.

> From Dr. John Wilson's *Cheerful Airs or Ballads*, 1660.

WHEN on mine eyes her eyes first shone,
    I all amazed
    Steadily gazed,
And she, to make me more amazed,
So caught, so wove, four eyes in one
As who had with advisement seen us
Would have admired Love's equal force between us.
But treason in those friendlike eyes,
    My heart first charming
    And then disarming,
So maimed it ere it dreamed of harming
As at her mercy now it lies,
And shows me to my endless smart
She loved but with her eyes, I with my heart.

> From Michael Este's *Madrigals*, 1604.

WHEN on my dear I do demand the due
    That to affection and firm faith belongeth,
A friend to me, she saith, she will be true,
    And with this answer still my joys prolongeth :
But, dear, tell me what friendship is in this,
Thus for to wrong me and delay my bliss?

From CAMPION *and* ROSSETER'S
Book of Airs, 1601.

WHEN the god of merry love
   As yet in his cradle lay,
Thus his withered nurse did say:
" Thou a wanton boy wilt prove
To deceive the powers above;
For by thy continual smiling
I see thy power of beguiling."

Therewith she the babe did kiss;
When a sudden fire outcame
From those burning lips of his
That did her with love inflame,
But none would regard the same:
So that, to her day of dying,
The old wretch lived ever crying.

From CAMPION *and* ROSSETER'S
Book of Airs, 1601.

WHEN to her lute Corinna sings,
   Her voice revives the leaden strings,
And doth in highest notes appear
As any challenged echo clear:
'But when she doth of mourning speak,
E'en with her sighs the strings do break.

And as her lute doth live or die,
Led by her passion, so must I :
For when of pleasure she doth sing,
My thoughts enjoy a sudden spring ;
But if she doth of sorrow speak,
E'en from my heart the strings do break.

From ROBERT JONES' *Ultimum Vale*, 1608.

WHEN will the fountain of my tears be dry,
    When will my sighs be spent?
When will desire agree to let me die?
    When will thy heart relent ?
It is not for my life I plead,
Since death the way to rest doth lead ;
      But stay for thy consent,
      Lest thou be discontent.

For if myself without thy leave I kill,
    My ghost will never rest ;
So hath it sworn to work thine only will
    And holds it ever best ;
For since it only lives by thee,
Good reason thou the ruler be :
      Then give me leave to die,
      And show thy power thereby.

From WILLIAM BYRD'S *Psalms,
Sonnets and Songs*, 1588.

WHERE Fancy fond for Pleasure pleads
    And Reason keeps poor Hope in jail,
There time it is to take my beads
And pray that Beauty may prevail;
Or else Despair will win the field
When Reason, Hope, and Pleasure yield.

My eyes presume to judge this case,
Whose judgment Reason doth disdain ;
But Beauty with her wanton face
Stands to defend the case is plain,
And at the bar of sweet Delight
She pleads that Fancy must be right.

But Shame will not have Reason yield,
Though Grief do swear it shall be so,
As though it were a perfect shield
To blush and fear to tell my woe :
When Silence force will at the last
To wish for wit when hope is past.

So far hath fond Desire outrun
The bo[u]nd which Reason set out first,
That, when Delight the fray begun,
I would now say, if that I durst,
That in her stead ten thousand Woes
Have sprung in field where Pleasure grows.

O that I might declare the rest
Of all the toys which Fancy turns
Like towers of wind within my breast,
Where fire is hid that never burns !
Then should I try one of the twain,
Either to love or to disdain.

But fine Conceit dares not declare
The strange conflict of Hope and Fear,
Lest Reason should be left so bare
That Love durst whisper in mine ear,
And tell me how my Fancy shall
Bring Reason to be Beauty's thrall.

I must therefore with silence build
The labyrinth of my delight,
Till love have tried in open field
Which of the twain shall win the fight :
I fear me Reason must give place
If Fancy fond win Beauty's grace.

From ROBERT JONES' *First Book
of Songs and Airs*, 1601.

WHERE lingering fear doth once possess the heart,
   There is the tongue
   Forced to prolong
And smother up his suit, while that his smart,
Like fire supprest, flames more in every part.

Who dares not speak deserves not his desire ;
    The boldest face
    Findeth most grace ;
Though women love that men should them admire,
They slily laugh at him dares come no higher.

Some think a glance, expressed by a sigh,
    Winning the field,
    Maketh them yield :
But while these glancing fools do roll the eye,
They beat the bush, away the bird doth flie.

A gentle heart in vertuous breast doth stay ;
    Pity doth dwell
    In Beauty's cell ;
A woman's heart doth not, though tongue, say "Nay:"
Repentance taught me this the other day.

Which had I wist, I presently had got
    The pleasing fruit
    Of my long suit ;
But Time hath now beguiled me of this lot,
For that by his foretop I took him not.

From Christ Church *MS.* L. L. 13.
(Music by JAMES HART.)

WHERE would coy Aminta run
    From a despairing lover's story ?
When her eyes have conquest won,
    Why should her ears refuse the glory ?

Should a slave, whom racks constrain,
Be forbidden to complain?
Let her scorn me, let her fly me,
Let her eyes their light deny me,
Ne'er shall my heart yield to despair
Or my tongue cease to tell my care.
Much to love, and much to pray,
Is to heaven the nearest way.

From RICHARD CARLTON'S *Madrigals*, 1601.

WHO vows devotion to fair beauty's shrine
  And leads a lover's life in pilgrimage,
Or that his constant faith may brighter shine
  Dwells days and nights in fancy's hermitage,
Shall find his truth's reward but loss of labour
Although he merit never so much favour.

From JOHN DOWLAND'S *First Book of Songs or Airs*, 1597. (Words by FULKE GREVILLE, LORD BROOKE.)

WHOEVER thinks or hopes of love for love,
  Or who beloved in Cupid's laws doth glory,
Who joys in vows or vows not to remove,
Who by this light god hath not been made sorry,—
Let him see me, eclipsed from my sun,
With dark clouds of an earth quite overrun.

Who thinks that sorrows felt, desires hidden,
Or humble faith in constant honour armed,
Can keep love from the fruit that is forbidden;
Who thinks that change is by entreaty charmed,—
Looking on me, let him know love's delights
Are treasures hid in caves but kept by sprites.

From JOHN DANYEL'S *Songs for
the Lute, Viol, and Voice,*
1606.

WHY canst thou not, as others do,
    Look on me with unwounding eyes?
And yet look sweet, but yet not so;
    Smile, but not in killing wise;
Arm not thy graces to confound;
Only look, but do not wound.

Why should mine eyes see more in you
    Than they can see in all the rest?
For I can others' beauties view,
    And not find my heart opprest.
O be as others are to me,
Or let me be more to thee.

From THOMAS RAVENSCROFT'S
Melismata, 1611.

The Courtier's Courtship to his Mistress.

WILL ye love me, lady sweet?
    You are young and love is meet.
Out alas! who then will sport thee?
Wanton yet in the spring:
Love is a pretty thing.
Kiss sweet as lovers do,
Prove kind to them that woo.

The Mistress to the Courtier.

Fie away, fie away! fie, fie, fie!
No, no, no, no, no, no, no, no, not I!
I'll live a maid till I be forty.

From ROBERT JONES' *First Book of Songs and Airs*, 1601.

WOMEN, what are they? Changing weather-cocks
That smallest puffs of lust have power to turn.
Women, what are they? Virtue's stumbling-blocks
Whereat weak fools do fall, the wiser spurn.
We men, what are we? Fools and idle boys
To spend our time in sporting with such toys.

Women, what are they? Trees whose outward rind
Makes show for fair when inward heart is hollow.
Women, what are they? Beasts of hyena's kind
That speak those fair'st whom most they mean to
    swallow.
We men, what are we? fools and idle boys
To spend our time in sporting with such toys.

Women, what are they? rocks upon the coast
Whereon we suffer shipwreck at our landing.
Women, what are they? patient creatures most
That rather yield than strive 'gainst aught with-
    standing.
We men, what are we? Fools and idle boys
To spend our time in sporting with such toys.

From WILLIAM BYRD'S Songs of
Sundry Natures, 1589.

WOUNDED I am, and dare not seek relief
    For this new stroke unseen but not unfelt:
No blood nor bruise is witness of my grief,
    But sighs and tears wherewith I mourn and melt.
If I complain, my witness is suspect;
    If I contain, with cares I am undone:
Sit still and die, tell truth and be reject:
    O hateful choice that sorrow cannot shun!
Yet of us twain whose loss shall be the less,
    Mine of my life or you of your good name?
Light is my death, regarding my distress,
    But your offence cries out to your defame,
"A virgin fair hath slain, for lack of grace,
The man that made an idol of her face!"

> From *Christ Church MS. K.* 3.
> 43-5. (Music by THOMAS
> FORD.)

YET[1] if his majesty our sovereign lord
  Should of his own accord
Friendly himself invite,
And say " I'll be your guest to morrow night,"
How should we stir ourselves, call and command
All hands to work ! " Let no man idle stand.
Set me fine Spanish tables in the hall,
  See they be fitted all ;
Let there be room to eat,
And order taken that there want no meat.
See every sconce and candlestick made bright,
That without tapers they may give a light.
Look to the presence : are the carpets spread,
  The dais[2] o'er the head,
The cushions in the chairs,
And all the candles lighted on the stairs?
Perfume the chambers, and in any case
Let each man give attendance in his place."
Thus if the king were coming would we do,
  And 'twere good reason too ;
For 'tis a duteous thing
To show all honour to an earthly king,
And after all our travail and our cost,
So he be pleased, to think no labour lost.

[1] These verses seem to have been taken from some longer poem.
[2] MS. "dazie."

But at the coming of the King of Heaven
All's set at six and seven :
We wallow in our sin,
Christ cannot find a chamber in the inn.
We entertain him always like a stranger,
And as at first still lodge him in the manger.

From FRANCIS PILKINGTON'S
Second Set of Madrigals,
1624.

YOU gentle nymphs that on these meadows play,
    And oft relate the loves of shepherds young,
Come sit you down, for, if you please to stay,
    Now may you hear an uncouth[1] passion sung :
A lad there is, and I am that poor groom,
That's fall'n in love and can not tell with whom.

From DR. JOHN WILSON'S *Cheerful Airs or Ballads,* 1660.

YOU say you love me, nay, can swear it too ;
    But stay, sir, 'twill not do.
I know you keep your oaths
Just as you wear your clothes,
While new and fresh in fashion ;
But once grown old,
You lay them by,
Forgot like words you speak in passion.
I'll not believe you, I.

[1] Strange, unaccustomed.

From FRANCIS PILKINGTON'S
First Book of Songs or Airs,
1605.

YOU that pine in long desire,
 Help me to cry,
"Come, love, come, love! quench this burning fire
 Lest through thy wound I die."

Hope that tires with vain delay
 Ever cries,
"Come, love, come, love! hours and years decay,
 In time Love's treasure dies.[1]"

All the day and all the night
 Still I call,
"Come, love, come, love!" but my dear delight
 Yields no relief at all.

Her unkindness scorns my moan
 That still shrikes,[2]
"Come, love, come, love! beauty pent alone
 Dies in her own dislikes."

[1] Old ed., "lyes."   [2] Shrieks.

From THOMAS CAMPION'S *Fourth
Book of Airs* (circ. 1617).

YOUNG and simple though I am
I have heard of Cupid's name,
Guess I can what thing it is
Men desire when they do kiss :
    Smoke can never burn, they say,
    But the flames that follow may.

I am not so foul or fair
To be proud or to despair ;
Yet[1] my lips have oft observed
Men that kiss them press them hard,
    As glad lovers use to do
    When their new-met loves they woo.

Faith, 'tis but a foolish mind,
Yet methinks a heat I find
Like thirst-longing, that doth bide
Ever on my weaker side,
    Where they say my heart doth move :
    Venus grant it be not love !

If it be, alas ! what then ?
Were not women made for men ?

---

[1] In this line and the next I have followed the text given in Ferrabosco's *Airs*, 1609.—In Campion's song-book we have a repetition of the lines "Guess I can . . . when they kiss" from the first stanza.

As good 'tis a thing were past,
That must needs be done at last :
   Roses that are overblown
   Grow less sweet, then fall alone.

Yet nor churl nor silken gull
Shall my maiden blossom pull :
Who shall not I soon can tell,
Who shall would I could as well :
   This I know, whoe'er he be,
   Love he must or flatter me.

From Thomas Weelkes
Madrigals, 1597.

YOUNG Cupid hath proclaimed a bloody war
   And vows revenge on all the maiden crew :
Oh yield, fair Chloris, lest in that foul jar
   Thine after penance makes thy folly rue.
And yet I fear, her wondrous beauty's such,
A thousand Cupids dare not Chloris touch.

From Thomas Campion's *Fourth
Book of Airs* (circ. 1617).

YOUR fair looks urge my desire :
      Calm it, sweet, with love !
   Stay ; O why will you retire ?
      Can you churlish prove ?

If love may persuade,
  Love's pleasures, dear, deny not :
Here is a grove secured with shade :
  O then be wise, and fly not.

Hark, the birds delighted sing,
  Yet our pleasure sleeps :
Wealth to none can profit bring,
  Which the miser keeps.
O come, while we may,
  Let's chain love with embraces ;
We have not all times time to stay,
  Nor safety in all places.

What ill find you now in this,
  Or who can complain ?
There is nothing done amiss
  That breeds no man pain.
'Tis now flow'ry May ;
  But even in cold December,
When all these leaves are blown away,
  This place shall I remember.

NOTES.

NOTES.

Page 1. "A feigned friend by proof I find."—Quaint old-fashioned moral verses (such as George Gascoigne or Tom Churchyard might have supplied in their rare moments of inspiration) were much affected by Byrd. The contents of his latest book—the collection of 1611—are mainly of a sententious or sacred character.

Page 4. "Are women fair and are they sweet?"— There is another, and fuller, version of this poem in Davison's "Poetical Rhapsody," where it is entitled "An Invective against Women," and bears the signature "Ignoto." See Sir Harris Nicolas' edition of the "Rhapsody," pp. 289-290.

Page 21. "Oh shake thy head, but *not a word but mum*."—The expression *not a word but mum* (=silence) was proverbial. Cf. Peele's "Old Wives' Tale":—

"What? *not a word but mum?* then, Sacrapant,
Thou art betrayed."

Page 24. "Dear, do not your fair beauty wrong."— This charming song is found in Thomas May's comedy "The Old Couple," 1658; but I strongly doubt whether he wrote it. Under the title of "Love's Prime" it had been included among the "Fancies and Fantastics" in "Wit's Recreations," 1640. It is also found in John Cotgrave's interesting and valuable anthology, "Wit's Interpreter," 1655.

Page 24. "Deceitful fancy, why delud'st thou me?" —The "Funeral Tears" are for the death of Charles Blount, Earl of Devonshire, husband of the famous Lady Penelope Rich. The composer's real name was plain John Cooper: he adopted the more sonorous name of Coperario (or Coprario) during his residence in Italy. See an excellent account of him (by Mr. Barclay Squire) in the "Dictionary of National Biography."

Page 33. "Farewell, dear love! since thou wilt needs be gone."—It is to this song that allusion is made in "Twelfth Night," ii. 3.

Page 37. "But die, poor wretch, shot through and through the *liver*."—The mention of the liver sounds inelegant to our ears; but the reader must remember that the liver was formerly supposed to be the seat of love. In that delightful book, "Batman upon Bartholomew," 1582, we are expressly told (on the authority of Isidorus) that "In the lyuer is the place of voluptuousnesse and lyking of the flesh" (lib. v. cap. 39).

Page 43. "She vows that they shall lead/ Apes in Avernus."—To lead apes in hell was the proverbial employment of old maids in the other world. William Corkine in his "Second Book of Airs," 1612, solemnly warns a young lady, who had vowed perpetual maidenhood, of the peril that she was running:—

> "O if you knew what chance to them befell
> That dance about with bobtail apes in hell,
> Yourself your virgin girdle would divide . . . .
> Rather than undergo such shame: no tongue can tell
> What injury is done to maids in hell."

Page 45. " Hey nonny no ! "—The " Mr. Gyles" whose name is subscribed to these verses was probably Nathaniel Giles, a musician of note. He was successively chorister at Magdalen, organist and master of the choristers at St. George's, Windsor, and master of the Children of the Chapel Royal. He died 24 January, 1633, and was buried at Windsor.

Page 51. " Pleased with a thought that endeth with a sigh."—The rhyme to "sigh" is "lieth"; but the irregularity is not so great as it seems, for the word " sigh " was frequently spelt " sight " and may easily have been pronounced " sigheth."

" I must complain, yet do enjoy my love."—In Christ Church MS. I. 5. 49 there is a copy of this song which differs considerably from the printed text. After the first stanza the MS. reads :—

> " Thus my complaints from her untruth arise,
> Accusing her and nature both in one ;
> For beauty stained is but a false disguise,
> A common wonder that is quickly gone,
> And false fair souls cannot, for all their feature,
> Without a true heart make a true fair creature.
>
> What need'[s]t thou plain if thou be still rejected?
> The fairest creature sometime may prove strange:
> Continual plaints will make thee still rejected
> If that her wanton mind be given to range:
> And nothing better fits a man's true parts
> Than to disdain t'encounter fair false hearts."

The song is also found (with the same text as in Campion's song-book) in Dowland's " Third Book of Songs or Airs," 1603.

Page 61. " Joy to the person of my love."—The MS. music-book (preserved in the Advocates' Library) in which this song occurs is a volume of some interest; but all, or nearly all, the songs that it contains are extant in printed copies. Several pieces are from the collections of Dowland, Campion, and other English composers. But the following little lyric I do not remember to have seen elsewhere:—

> "All my wits hath will enwrapped,
> All my sense desire entrapped;
> All my faith to fancy fixed,
> All my joys to love amixed:
>   All my love I offer thee,
>   Once for all yet look on me.
>
> Let me see thy heavenly feature:
> O heavens what a heavenly creature!
> All the powers of heaven preserve thee!
> Love himself hath sworn to serve thee.
>   Princess in a goddess' place,
>   Blessed be that Angel's face!
>
> Look how Love thy servant dieth,
> Hark how Hope for comfort crieth:
> Take some pity on poor fancy,
> Let not fancy prove a frenzy:
>   Comfort this poor heart of mine:
>   Love and I and all are thine."

The text of the English songs in the volume has been slightly Scotticised in some instances. At a later date Tom D'Urfey's songs were similarly treated (as Mr. Ebsworth has abundantly shown) by lettered Scots. (I have used the third edition of Forbes' "Cantus," 1682. The very rare first edition, 1661, I have never seen.)

Page 66. "Lock up, fair lids," &c.—This song is also found (with some slight textual variations) in Vautor's "Airs," 1619.

Page 68. " Love in thy youth, fair maid."—This song is printed in Beloe's "Anecdotes," where it is said to be taken from Walter Porter's "Madrigals and Airs," 1632. I have searched far and wide for this song-book, but have never been fortunate enough to see a copy. There is an early manuscript copy of the present song (without music) in Ashmole MS. 38, No. 188.

Page 69. " Lovely shepherd, ope thine eye."—I am not aware that this dainty dialogue has ever been printed. Possibly it is from some lost masque.

Page 84. "Of Neptune's empire let us sing."—These verses are printed in Davison's "Poetical Rhapsody," with the heading "This Hymn was sung by Amphitrite, Thamesis, and other Sea-Nymphs, in Gray's Inn Masque, at the Court, 1594." See Sir Harris Nicolas' edition of the "Rhapsody," pp. 271, 364.

Page 90. "Rest awhile, you cruel cares."—The word "ever" in the seventh line of this song is otiose and should doubtless be omitted.

Page 98. "So saith my fair and beautiful Lycoris."—This is a rendering of an Italian madrigal of Luca Marenzio. In the former series I gave another version ("Thus saith my Chloris bright") from Wilbye's "Madrigals," 1598.

Page 106. "The *fountains* smoke, and yet no flames they show."—Surely *fountains* must be a misprint for *mountains*.

Page 114. " Thou sent'st to me a heart was crowned."—I seem to have met these verses in print somewhere, but cannot at the moment trace them. For neatness and elegance they are worthy of Ben Jonson.

Page 116. "Thyrsis and Milla, arm in arm together."

—In Harl. MS. 791, fol. 55, there is a poem (beginning "A silly swain that long had loved a lass") partly identical with this song of Morley's. The MS. poem concludes—

> "'O fool!' quoth she; and so burst out in laughter,
> Blushed, ran away, and scorned him ever after."

I should like to give the MS. text entire; but some of the verses are written with a freedom that would shock sensitive ears.

Page 129. "What . . . conversing."—Here again we find Campion repeating the word "conversing" of l. 1 at the end of l. 3. The text may be corrupt; but I suspect that the repetition was intentional. Minor poets must be careful about their rhymes; but Campion may well be allowed to take his own course. How tender and beautiful are the second and third stanzas!

Page 134. "When I was born Lucina *cross-legged* sat," *i.e.* to prolong the pangs of child-birth and hinder the child's entrance to the world. Witches were frequently accused of sitting cross-legged at the door of travailing women.

Page 143. "*Women*, what are they?—*We men*, what are we?"—The play on the words *women* and *we men* was greatly relished by our old poets. Cf. Peele's "Edward I." :—

> "*Lancaster.* Believe him not, sweet niece : *we men* can speak smooth for advantage.
> *Joan. Women*, do you mean, my good uncle? Well, be the accent where it will, women are women."

Page 145. "Yet if his majesty," &c.—In the MS.

these fine verses are followed by Shakespeare's "Sigh no more, ladies," set to music by Thomas Ford.

Page 148. "Young and simple though I am."—There is a copy of this song in Advocates' MS. 5. 2. 14. It concludes with the following additional stanza :—

> "Married wives may take or leave;
> When they list, refuse, receive;
> We poor maids may not do so,
> We must answer Ay with No:
> We must seem strange, coy, and curst,
> Yet do we would fain if we durst."

LIST OF SONG-BOOKS.

AMNER, JOHN. *Sacred Hymns*, 1615. Page 2.
ATTEY, JOHN. *First Book of Airs*, 1622. 56, 106.
BARLEY, WILLIAM. *New Book of Tabliture*, 1596.
    112.
BARTLET, JOHN. *Airs*, 1606. 50, 107, 132.
BATESON, THOMAS. *First Set of English Madrigals*,
    1604. 31, 72, 100.
    Second Set of Madrigals, 1618. 15, 23, 37, 45, 49,
    53, 73, 86, 102, 107.
BYRD, WILLIAM. *Psalms, Sonnets and Songs*, 1588.
    3, 16, 57, 138.
    Songs of Sundry Natures, 1589. 4, 54, 144.
    Psalms, Songs, and Sonnets, 1611. 1, 105.
CAMPION, THOMAS. *Gesta Graiorum. Grays Inn
    Masque*, 1594. 84.
    *Description of a Masque presented before the King's
    Majesty at Whitehall*, 1607. 75, 78.
    Two Books of Airs [circ. 1613]. 18, 19, 30, 41,
    46, 110, 120, 126.
    Third Book of Airs [circ. 1617]. 10, 12, 54, 97,
    129.
    Fourth Book of Airs. 51, 68, 80, 90, 98, 113, 125,
    148, 149.
CAMPION, THOMAS, and ROSSETER, PHILIP. *Book of*

Airs, 1601. 13, 36, 42, 48, 55, 59, 89, 93, 104, 115, 121, 136.
CARLTON, RICHARD. *Madrigals*, 1601. 22, 56, 66, 110, 141.
COPERARIO, JOHN. *Funeral Tears*, 1606. 24, 82.
CORKINE, WILLIAM. *Airs*, 1610. 102.
 Second Book of Airs, 1612. 94, 95, 121, 134.
DANYEL, JOHN. *Songs for the Lute, Viol, and Voice*, 1606. 52, 117, 128, 142.
DOWLAND, JOHN. *First Book of Songs or Airs*, 1597. 9, 90, 123, 141.
 Second Book of Songs or Airs, 1600. 21, 71, 76, 118.
 Third Book of Songs or Airs, 1603. 35, 83, 92.
 A Pilgrim's Solace, 1612. 26, 38.
ESTE, MICHAEL. *Madrigals*, 1604. 31, 97, 119, 135.
FARNABY, GILES. *Canzonets*, 1598. 100.
FERRABOSCO, ALFONSO. *Airs*, 1609. 29, 104.
FORBES, JOHN. *Cantus, Songs and Fancies*, 1661. 61.
GIBBONS, ORLANDO. *First Set of Madrigals*, 1612. 32, 64, 74, 120.
GREAVES, THOMAS. *Songs of Sundry Kinds*, 1604. 64.
HILTON, JOHN. *Airs*, 1627. 114.
JONES, ROBERT. *First Book of Songs and Airs*, 1601. 33, 65, 81, 88, 128, 134, 139, 143.
 Second Book of Songs and Airs, 1601. 25, 32, 35.
 First Set of Madrigals, 1607. 67, 96, 112.
 Ultimum Vale, 1608. 7, 17, 26, 28, 95, 101, 137.
 Musical Dream, 1609. 3, 51, 72, 133.
 The Muses' Garden of Delights, 1610. 47, 60, 85, 99, 106, 108.
KIRBYE, GEORGE. *First Set of English Madrigals*. 2.

MORLEY, THOMAS. *Introduction to Practical Music*, 1597. 96.
    First Book of Airs, 1600. 21, 70, 116.
    First Book of Ballets, 1600. 130.
    Madrigals, 1600. 85.
Musica Transalpina. The Second Book of Madrigals, 1597. 98.
PEERSON, MARTIN. *Private Music*, 1620. 15, 20, 58, 66, 67, 82, 87, 109, 124.
PILKINGTON, FRANCIS. *First Book of Songs or Airs*, 1605. 11, 79, 147.
    First Set of Madrigals, 1614. 94.
    Second Set of Madrigals, 1624. 146.
PORTER, WALTER. *Madrigals and Airs*, 1632. 68.
RAVENSCROFT, THOMAS. *Pammelia*, 1609. 43.
    Melismata, 1611. 143.
ROBINSON, THOMAS. *New Cithern Lessons*, 1609. 77.
SMITH, STAFFORD. *Musica Antiqua*. 24.
VAUTOR, THOMAS. *Songs of Divers Airs and Natures*, 1619. 14, 123.
WEELKES, THOMAS. *Madrigals*, 1597. 2, 113, 149.
    Madrigals of five and six parts, 1600. 76, 115.
    Madrigals of Six Parts, 1600. 116.
    Airs or Fantastic Spirits, 1608. 119.
WILBYE, JOHN. *Second Set of Madrigals*, 1609. 18, 100.
WILSON, DR. JOHN. *Cheerful Airs or Ballads*, 1660. 38, 39, 131, 132, 135, 146.

Add. MS. 10,338. Page 69.
    15,117. 91.
    17,790-2. 14, 73, 127.
    18,936. 88.

Christ Church MS. I. 1. 13.   140.
   I. 4. 78.   122, 125.
   I. 5. 49.   6, 20, 23, 45, 111.
   K. 3. 43-7.   4, 65, 74, 103, 107, 145.
Mus. Sch. MS. F. 575.   46, 56, 114.

CHISWICK PRESS :—C. WHITTINGHAM AND CO., TOOKS COURT,
CHANCERY LANE.

LONDON,
14 KING WILLIAM STREET, STRAND, W.C.

JOHN C. NIMMO'S
AUTUMN LIST OF NEW BOOKS
FOR
OCTOBER 1887.

A NEW ILLUSTRATED WORK BY THE AUTHOR OF
"FLEMISH INTERIORS."

In large crown 8vo. With One Hundred Illustrations by R. CAULFIELD ORPEN. Cloth elegant, gilt top, price 7s. 6d.

"De Omnibus Rebus."
AN OLD MAN'S DISCURSIVE RAMBLINGS ON THE ROAD OF EVERYDAY LIFE.
By the Author of "Flemish Interiors."
With One Hundred Illustrations by R. CAULFIELD ORPEN.

NOTE.—These pages are written in the character of a shrewd, observant, and perhaps satirical, but not ill-natured, old bachelor who knows how to find in his journeyings, by omnibus or otherwise, matter for reflection and comment, and who communicates familiarly his impressions of men and things, turning them about so as to get at their humorous, their practical, and their pathetic aspect. With these he mingles past and present experiences of life, congenial episodes, and representative types of character as they suggest themselves to his memory; but his gossip is always popular in character, bearing on subjects of social economy and contemporary ethics necessarily interesting to our common humanity.

New Historical Work by F. G. Lee, D.D.

Large crown 8vo, cloth, price 8s. 6d.

REGINALD POLE,
CARDINAL ARCHBISHOP OF CANTERBURY.

AN HISTORICAL SKETCH. WITH AN INTRODUCTORY PROLOGUE AND PRACTICAL EPILOGUE BY

FREDERICK GEORGE LEE, D.D.

With an Etched Portrait of Cardinal Pole.

NOTE.—This volume, besides dealing with the life and character of Cardinal Pole, will specially set forth the nature of his great work as an ecclesiastical statesman and diplomatist,—unpublished details of which will be provided from the Archives of the Vatican, his Register at Lambeth, and various publications and letters of himself and his contemporaries. Incidentally, the further policy of Queen Mary and her great statesman, Bishop Gardiner, will be dealt with; as also the personal characteristics of the Queen herself, and some of the chief Englishmen of Pole's era.

New Volumes of the Elizabethan Dramatists Series.

In Two Volumes, post 8vo, cloth, price 7s. 6d. per vol. *net.*
Also fine large paper copies, medium 8vo, cloth.

THE WORKS OF GEORGE PEELE.
Edited by A. H. BULLEN, B.A.

NOTE.—A new *Library Edition* of Peele's works is needed; for Pickering's beautiful volumes are rare and costly. In the present edition some interesting facsimiles of title-pages, &c., will be given.

A New Volume of Elizabethan Lyrics.

Post 8vo, hand-made paper, 750 copies, each numbered, price 10s. 6d. *net.*
Also 250 large paper copies, in half German calf, each numbered.

More Lyrics from the Song-Books of the Elizabethan Age.
Edited by A. H. BULLEN, B.A.

NOTE.—Many of the poems in this collection are from unique books preserved in the British Museum, the Bodleian Library, the Royal College of Music, and Mr. Halliwell-Phillipps' Library at Hollingbury Copse. Others are printed, for the first time, from MSS. The Editor has been careful to include only such songs as are "choicely good."

14 King William Street, Strand, London, W.C.

Small 4to, Two Volumes, handsomely bound in half-German calf, gilt top, price 36s. *net.*
Also 100 copies on fine super royal 8vo paper.

The Life of Benvenuto Cellini.

NEWLY TRANSLATED INTO ENGLISH.

By JOHN ADDINGTON SYMONDS.

With Portrait and Eight Etchings by F. LAGUILLERMIE.

Also Eighteen reproductions of the Works of the Master, printed in Gold, Silver, and Bronze.

---

500 copies of this Edition printed for England and 250 for America.

NOTE.—A book which the great Goethe thought worthy of translating into German with the pen of *Faust* and *Wilhelm Meister*, a book which Auguste Comte placed upon his very limited list for the perusal of reformed humanity, is one with which we have the right to be occupied, not once or twice, but over and over again. It cannot lose its freshness. What attracted the encyclopædic minds of men so different as Comte and Goethe to its pages still remains there. This attractive or compulsive quality, to put the matter briefly, is the flesh and blood reality of Cellini's self-delineation. A man stands before us in his *Memoirs* unsophisticated, unimbellished, with all his native faults upon him, and with all his potent energies portrayed in the veracious manner of Velasquez, with bold strokes and animated play of light and colour. His autobiography is the record of action and passion. Suffering, enjoying, enduring, working with restless activity; hating, loving, hovering from place to place as impulse moves him; the man presents himself dramatically by his deeds and spoken words, never by his pondering or meditative broodings. It is this healthy externality which gives its great charm to Cellini's self-portrayal, and renders it an imperishable document for the student of human nature.

---

14 King William Street, Strand, London, W.C.

NEW ILLUSTRATED EDITION OF DR. DORAN'S GREAT WORK.

In Three Volumes, demy 8vo, Roxburghe binding,
gilt top, price 54s. *net.*
Also large paper copies, royal 8vo, with Portraits in duplicate.

"THEIR MAJESTIES' SERVANTS."

ANNALS OF THE ENGLISH STAGE

FROM

THOMAS BETTERTON TO EDMUND KEAN.

By DR. DORAN, F.S.A.

Edited and Revised by R. W. LOWE from Author's
Annotated Copy.

With Fifty Copperplate Portraits and Eighty Wood Engravings.

NOTE.—The following are some of the chief features of this new edited and revised edition of Dr. Doran's well-known work.

It is illustrated for the first time with fifty newly engraved copperplate portraits of the leading and best known actors and actresses, all of which are printed as India proofs.

There are also fifty-six illustrations, newly engraved on wood, printed on fine Japanese paper, and mounted at the head of each chapter, as well as some twenty or more character illustrations, also newly engraved on wood, and printed with the text at end of the chapters.

There are numerous new and original footnotes given, as well as a copious and exhaustive Index to each volume.

Besides the demy 8vo edition, a limited number will be printed on royal 8vo, fine deckle-edged paper, with a duplicate set of the fifty portraits, one on Japanese paper and the other on plate paper, as India proofs.

Each of these copies will be numbered.

14 King William Street, Strand, London, W.C.

A Bibliography of Theatrical Literature.

In demy 8vo, 400 pages, cloth, price 18s. *net*. Also, One Hundred Copies on fine deckle-edge royal 8vo paper, each numbered.

A BIBLIOGRAPHICAL ACCOUNT

OF

ENGLISH THEATRICAL LITERATURE

FROM

THE EARLIEST TIMES TO THE PRESENT DAY.

By ROBERT W. LOWE.

NOTE.—There is as yet no Bibliography of the general literature of the stage. Plays have been catalogued many times, and some of our greatest bibliographers have directed their attention to Shakespearian literature; but no attempt has been made to give even the baldest catalogue of the large and curious mass of books relating to the History of the Stage, the Biography of Actors and Actresses, the Controversy regarding the Influence of the Stage, the numerous curious Theatrical Trials, and the many scandalous attacks on the personal character of celebrated performers. In the last two classes especially there are many curious pamphlets dealing with the strangest scandals, and often containing the most disgraceful accusations, of which no account is to be found except in the originals themselves, which, having been in many cases suppressed, are of extreme rarity.

The present work is intended to supply in some measure the want which has been felt by all writers on theatrical subjects, as well as by all collectors of theatrical books. It consists of about 2000 titles, the great majority of which are taken directly from the works described. These will be arranged alphabetically, with exhaustive cross-references. Notes regarding each actor and actress will be given, and also an account of the occurrences to which particular works refer, special attention being paid to the less known and more curious pamphlets. Thus, it is hoped, the work will have a historical as well as bibliographical value, and will form a History of the Stage, especially in those details of which regular histories take little or no cognisance. Plays will be excluded, except where they have prefaces, &c., of historical or controversial interest; and of Shakespeariana, only such works will be included as relate to the performance of Shakespeare's plays or the representation of his characters by particular actors.

Quotations of prices at recent famous sales will be given, and the rarity of scarce books will be pointed out.

14 King William Street, Strand, London, W.C.

Third Edition, newly Revised and Corrected, and greatly Enlarged, in 2 vols. medium 8vo, cloth, Three Hundred Engravings and Twelve Full-Page Plates, price 21s.

THE ROSICRUCIANS:
THEIR RIGHTS AND MYSTERIES.
By HARGRAVE JENNINGS.

Allen's Indian Mail.

"Valuable, interesting, and instructive, the work teaches how dangerous it is to condemn what is not understood, or to criticise what is imperfectly realised. Liberality of judgment should be the motto of mankind in these days of intelligence and enlightenment, and a study of the mysterious will clear the path in this direction from many of the notions conceived in intolerance and nurtured in hardness of heart. Read, gentle reader, and be wise!"

Uniform with A. H. BULLEN'S "*Lyrics from the Song-Books of the Elizabethan Age.*"

Post 8vo, hand-made paper, 500 copies, each numbered, price 10s. 6d. *net*. Also 250 copies, large paper, in half-German calf, each numbered.

ENGLAND'S HELICON.
A COLLECTION OF LYRICAL POEMS PUBLISHED IN 1600.
Edited by A. H. BULLEN.

The Spectator.

"With what pleasure would Leigh Hunt, Hazlitt, or Charles Lamb have taken into their hands this new edition of the Elizabethan song-book, 'England's Helicon;' and how gladly would they acknowledge the influence of sixty years, the advance in taste, themselves its leaders, which will win for such a book delight and admiration, rather than 'patronage!' The book consists of a collection of lyrical and pastoral poems, and the modern editor, who, one need hardly say, has done his work with perfect care and taste, has prefaced the poems with an introduction telling us all we want to know about almost every one of them."

Imperial 8vo, half-bound crushed morocco, price 21s.

REYNARD THE FOX.
AFTER THE GERMAN VERSION OF GOETHE.
By THOMAS JAMES ARNOLD, Esq.

With Sixty Illustrations from the Designs of WILHELM VON KAULBACH, and Twelve India Proof Steel Engravings by JOSEPH WOLF.

NOTE.—One of the specialities of the present edition consists in the illustrations, faithfully engraved by English artists from the designs of Kaulbach, as well as twelve clever full-page steel engravings by Augustus Fox, from the drawings of Joseph Wolf.

Saturday Review.

"We are more concerned with the engravers' skill, the veracity with which Kaulbach's rich fancy and racy humour are reproduced, together with the congenial spirit of Mr. Wolf's clever drawings, and in these essential particulars the present edition is worthy of warm commendation."

THE NEW EDITED AND COMPLETE EDITIONS
OF
The Elizabethan Dramatists.

This is the first instalment towards a collective edition of the Dramatists who lived about the time of Shakespeare. The type will be distributed after each work is printed.

One of the chief features of this New Edition of the Elizabethan Dramatists, besides the handsome and handy size of the volumes, will be the fact that *each Work will be carefully edited and new notes given throughout.*

ALGERNON CHARLES SWINBURNE
(IN THE *NINETEENTH CENTURY*, JANUARY 1886)

ON THE

Elizabethan Dramatists.

"If it be true, as we are told on high authority, that the greatest glory of England is her literature, and the greatest glory of English literature is its poetry, it is not less true that the greatest glory of English poetry lies rather in its dramatic than its epic or its lyric triumphs. The name of Shakespeare is above the names even of Milton and Coleridge and Shelley; and the names of his comrades in art and their immediate successors are above all but the highest names in any other province of our song. There is such an overflowing life, such a superb exuberance of abounding and exulting strength, in the dramatic poetry of the half century extending from 1590 to 1640, that all other epochs of English literature seem as it were but half awake and half alive by comparison with this generation of giants and of gods. There is more sap in this than in any other branch of the national bay-tree; it has an energy in fertility which reminds us rather of the forest than the garden or the park. It is true that the weeds and briars of the underwood are but too likely to embarrass and offend the feet of the rangers and the gardeners who trim the level flower-plots or preserve the domestic game of enclosed and ordered lowlands in the tamer demesnes of literature. The sun is strong and the wind sharp in the climate which reared the fellows and the followers of Shakespeare. The extreme inequality and roughness of the ground must also be taken into account when we are disposed, as I for one have often been disposed, to wonder beyond measure at the apathetic ignorance of average students in regard of the abundant treasure to be gathered from this widest and most fruitful province in the poetic empire of England. And yet, since Charles Lamb threw open its gates to all comers in the ninth year of the present century, it cannot but seem strange that comparatively so few should have availed themselves of the entry to so rich and royal an estate. Mr. Bullen has taken up a task than which none more arduous and important, none worthier of thanks and praise, can be undertaken by any English scholar."

14 King William Street, Strand, London, W.C.

Volumes now Ready of the new Edited and Complete Editions of the Elizabethan Dramatists.

Post 8vo, cloth. Published price, 7s. 6d. per volume *net*; also large fine-paper edition, medium 8vo, cloth.

The following are Edited by A. H. BULLEN, B.A.:—

THE WORKS OF GEORGE PEELE.	Two Volumes.
THE WORKS OF JOHN MARSTON.	Three Volumes.
THE WORKS OF THOMAS MIDDLETON.	Eight Volumes.
THE WORKS OF CHRISTOPHER MARLOWE.	Three Volumes.

Others in active preparation.

SOME PRESS NOTICES.

Athenæum.—"Mr. Bullen's edition deserves warm recognition. It is intelligent, scholarly, adequate. His preface is judicious. The elegant edition of the Dramatists of which these volumes are the first is likely to stand high in public estimation. . . . The completion of the series will be a boon to bibliographers and scholars alike."

Saturday Review.—"Mr. Bullen has discharged his task as editor in all important points satisfactorily, his introduction is well informed and well written, and his notes are well chosen and sufficient. . . . We hope it may be his good fortune to give and ours to receive every Dramatist, from Peele to Shirley, in this handsome, convenient, and well-edited form."

The Spectator.—"Probably one of the boldest literary undertakings of our time, on the part of publisher as well as editor, is the fine edition of the Dramatists which has been placed in Mr. Bullen's careful hands; considering the comprehensiveness of the subject, and the variety of knowledge it demands, the courage of the editor is remarkable."

Notes and Queries.—". . . Appropriately, then, the series Mr. Bullen edits and Mr. Nimmo issues in most attractive guise is headed by Marlowe, the leader, and in some respects all but the mightiest spirit, of the great army of English Dramatists."

The Academy.—"Mr. Bullen is known to all those interested in such things as an authority on most matters connected with old plays. We are not surprised, therefore, to find these volumes well edited throughout. They are not overburdened with notes."

Scotsman.—"Never in the history of the world has a period been marked by so much of literary power and excellence as the Elizabethan period; and never have the difficulties in the way of literature seemed to be greater. The three volumes which Mr. Nimmo has issued now may be regarded as earnests of more to come, and as proofs of the excellence which will mark this edition of the Elizabethan Dramatists as essentially the best that has been published. Mr. Bullen is a competent editor in every respect."

The Standard.—"Throughout Mr. Bullen has done his difficult work remarkably well, and the publisher has produced it in a form which will make the edition of early Dramatists of which it is a part an almost indispensable addition to a well-stocked library."

Pall Mall Gazette.—". . . If the series is continued as it is begun, by one of the most careful editors, this set of the English Dramatists will be a coveted literary possession."

Daily Telegraph.—"The introduction to this new edition of Marston is of exceeding interest, and is honourable to the earnest spirit in which Mr. Bullen is steadfastly pursuing the object set before him in this notable series."

14 King William Street, Strand, London, W.C.

Standard Historical Works.

*Twelve Volumes, demy 8vo, cloth, uncut edges, price £5, 5s. net;
also in Tree calf, gilt top, Rivière's binding.*

THE WORKS OF

The Right Hon. Edmund Burke.

WITH ENGRAVED PORTRAIT FROM THE PAINTING

By Sir JOSHUA REYNOLDS.

Carefully Revised and Collated with the Latest Editions.

NOTE.—The publication of this COMPLETE LIBRARY EDITION of the Writings and Speeches of a great Writer and Orator, whose works have been so frequently quoted of late in the British Houses of Parliament, the publisher feels may be opportune to many readers and admirers of one of the greatest of the sons of men. Viewed in the light of the present age, how great is our admiration of that foresight which foretold, and that wisdom which would have averted, the storms which menaced the peace and well-being of his country! His public labours present a continuous struggle against the stupidity, the obstinacy, and the venality of the politicians of his day.

So long as virtue shall be beloved, wisdom revered, or genius admired, so long will the memory of this illustrious exemplar of all be fresh in the world's history; for human nature has too much interest in the preservation of such a character ever to permit the name of EDMUND BURKE to perish from the earth.

CONTENTS.

Vindication of Natural Society.	Hints for an Essay on the Drama.
The Sublime and Beautiful.	An Essay towards an Abridgment of the English History.
Observations on a Late Publication on "The Present State of the Nation."	Papers on India.
	Articles of Charge against Warren Hastings.
Thoughts on the Cause of the Present Discontents.	Speeches in the Impeachment of Warren Hastings.
Reflections on the Revolution in France.	Miscellaneous Speeches.
Thoughts on French Affairs.	Letters.
Thoughts and Details on Scarcity.	Index, &c.

14 King William Street, Strand, London, W.C.

STANDARD HISTORICAL WORKS—continued.

Medium 8vo, fine paper, with Four Etched Portraits, &c., cloth,
21s. *net.*

The Autobiography of Edward,
LORD HERBERT OF CHERBURY.

WITH INTRODUCTION, NOTES, APPENDICES, AND A CONTINUATION OF THE LIFE.

By SYDNEY L. LEE, B.A., Balliol College, Oxford.

Notes and Queries.

"Lord Herbert's autobiography is an absolute masterpiece, worthy of the place assigned it by Mr. Swinburne among the best one hundred books. Quite fascinating are the records of adventure Lord Herbert supplies, and the book, when once the preliminary statement of pedigree, &c., is got over, will be read to the last line by every reader of taste. A new lease of popularity is conferred upon it by the handsome and scholarly reprint Mr. Lee has given to the world. The volume itself belongs to the series of library reprints of Mr. Nimmo, which are simply the most attractive of the day. Mr. Lee, meanwhile, has executed in the most scrupulous, careful, and competent manner the task of editing."

Medium 8vo, fine paper, with Four Etched Portraits, &c., cloth,
21s. *net.*

The Life of William Cavendish,
DUKE OF NEWCASTLE,

To which is added the TRUE RELATION OF MY BIRTH, BREEDING, AND LIFE.

By MARGARET, DUCHESS OF NEWCASTLE.

EDITED BY C. H. FIRTH, M.A.

Saturday Review.

"The book is, without doubt, a pleasant one. In the midst of the stony-hearted Restoration, its naïve enthusiasm, its quaint and embroidered eloquence, its flavour of a bygone day, give it a curious charm. It is like a Shirley flourishing on into the age of Shadwell and Etherege."

The Scotsman.

"It has a distinct value as a contemporary picture of the life, modes of thought, and habits of a great Royalist nobleman, who played a prominent part in some of the most memorable episodes of English history."

---

14 King William Street, Strand, London, W.C.

STANDARD HISTORICAL WORKS—continued.

Medium 8vo, fine paper, with Ten Etched Portraits, &c., cloth, Two Volumes, 42s. net.

MEMOIRS OF THE LIFE OF COLONEL HUTCHINSON.

By his Widow, LUCY.

REVISED AND EDITED BY CHARLES H. FIRTH, M.A.

Athenæum.

"Is an excellent edition of a famous book. Mr. Firth presents the 'Memoirs' with a modernised orthography and a revised scheme of punctuation. He retains the notes of Julius Hutchinson, and supplements them by annotations —corrective and explanatory—of his own. Since their publication in 1805, the 'Memoirs' have been a kind of classic. To say that this is the best and fullest edition of them in existence is to say everything."

Medium 8vo, fine paper, Roxburghe binding, gilt top, and Two Etchings, price 15s.

A Chronicle History of the Life and Work of William Shakespeare.

PLAYER, POET, AND PLAYMAKER.

By F. G. FLEAY, M.A.

From Professor A. W. Ward's Preface to the Second Edition of Marlowe's "Dr. Faustus."

"Mr. Fleay's new Life of Shakespeare will, in my opinion, before long be acknowledged as one of the most important works on the history of the Elizabethan drama which this age has produced."

Extract from a Letter to the Author from Dr. H. H. Furness.

"The man himself was always unreal to me, and I never could bring myself to believe that he ever really existed. But your book has left upon me the impression, as deep as it is strange, that such a man did really live, and that he belonged to the noble army of workers.

"I had confidence in you and followed holding your hand, at times lost in wonder and admiration over the miraculous memory and indefatigable research of my guide."

---

14 King William Street, Strand, London, W.C.

STANDARD HISTORICAL WORKS—continued.

Copyright Edition, with Ten Etched Portraits. In Ten Vols., demy 8vo, cloth, £5, 5s. *net*.

Lingard's History of England.

FROM THE FIRST INVASION BY THE ROMANS TO THE ACCESSION OF WILLIAM AND MARY IN 1688.

By JOHN LINGARD, D.D.

This New Copyright Library Edition of "Lingard's History of England," besides containing all the latest notes and emendations of the Author, with Memoir, is enriched with Ten Portraits, newly etched by Damman, of the following personages, viz.:—Dr. Lingard, Edward I., Edward III., Cardinal Wolsey, Cardinal Pole, Elizabeth, James I., Cromwell, Charles II., James II.

The Times.

"No greater service can be rendered to literature than the republication, in a handsome and attractive form, of works which time and the continued approbation of the world have made classical. . . . The accuracy of Lingard's statements on many points of controversy, as well as the genial sobriety of his view, is now recognised."

The Tablet.

"It is with the greatest satisfaction that we welcome this new edition of Dr. Lingard's 'History of England.' It has long been a desideratum. . . . No general history of England has appeared which can at all supply the place of Lingard, whose painstaking industry and careful research have dispelled many a popular delusion, whose candour always carries his reader with him, and whose clear and even style is never fatiguing."

The Spectator.

"We are glad to see that the demand for Dr. Lingard's *England* still continues. Few histories give the reader the same impression of exhaustive study. This new edition is excellently printed, and illustrated with ten portraits of the greatest personages in our history."

Dublin Review.

"It is pleasant to notice that the demand for Lingard continues to be such that publishers venture on a well-got-up library edition like the one before us. More than sixty years have gone since the first volume of the first edition was published; many equally pretentious histories have appeared during that space, and have more or less disappeared since, yet Lingard lives—is still a recognised and respected authority."

The Scotsman.

"There is no need, at this time of day, to say anything in vindication of the importance, as a standard work, of Dr. Lingard's 'History of England.' . . . Its intrinsic merits are very great. The style is lucid, pointed, and puts no strain upon the reader; and the printer and publisher have neglected nothing that could make this—what it is likely long to remain—the standard edition of a work of great historical and literary value."

Daily Telegraph.

"True learning, untiring research, a philosophic temper, and the possession of a graphic, pleasing style were the qualities which the author brought to his task, and they are displayed in every chapter of his history."

14 King William Street, Strand, London, W.C.

STANDARD HISTORICAL WORKS—continued.

Two Volumes, 8vo, Sixty-four Portraits, Roxburghe binding, gilt top, price 30s. *net*.

MEMOIRS OF COUNT GRAMMONT.

By ANTHONY HAMILTON.

A NEW EDITION, EDITED, WITH NOTES, BY SIR WALTER SCOTT.

With Sixty-four Portraits Engraved by EDWARD SCRIVEN.

Hallam.

"The 'Memoirs of Grammont,' by Anthony Hamilton, scarcely challenge a place as historical; but we are now looking more at the style than the intrinsic importance of books. Every one is aware of the peculiar felicity and fascinating gaiety which they display."

T. B. Macaulay.

"The artist to whom we owe the most highly finished and vividly coloured picture of the English Court in the days when the English Court was gayest."

Medium 8vo, fine paper, Eighty-eight Illustrations, cloth, gilt top, price 21s. *net*.

OLD TIMES:

A PICTURE OF SOCIAL LIFE AT THE END OF THE EIGHTEENTH CENTURY.

COLLECTED AND ILLUSTRATED FROM THE SATIRICAL AND OTHER SKETCHES OF THE DAY.

By JOHN ASHTON.

Author of "Social Life in the Reign of Queen Anne."

With Eighty-eight Illustrations.

Daily Telegraph.

"That is the best and truest history of the past which comes nearest to the life of the bulk of the people. It is in this spirit that Mr. John Ashton has composed 'Old Times,' intended to be a picture of social life at the end of the eighteenth century. The illustrations form a very valuable, and at the same time quaint and amusing, feature of the volume."

Saturday Review.

"'Old Times,' however, is not only valuable as a book to be taken up for a few minutes at a time; a rather careful reading will repay those who wish to brush up their recollections of the period. To some extent it may serve as a book of reference, and even historians may find in it some useful matter concerning the times of which it treats. The book is in every respect suited for a hall or library table in a country house."

STANDARD HISTORICAL WORKS—continued.

THE MONKS OF THE WEST,

FROM ST. BENEDICT TO ST. BERNARD.

By the COUNT DE MONTALEMBERT,
Member of the French Academy.

Authorised Translation. Seven Volumes 8vo, cloth, £4, 4s. *net.*

(*Published by* Messrs. W. BLACKWOOD & SONS, *Edinburgh.*)

CONTENTS OF THE WORK.

Introduction.
The Roman Empire after the Peace of the Church.
Monastic Precursors in the East.
Monastic Precursors in the West.
St. Benedict.
St. Gregory the Great — Monastic Italy and Spain in the Sixth and Seventh Centuries.
The Monks under the First Merovingians.
St. Columbanus—The Irish in Gaul and the Colonies of Luxeuil.
Christian Origin of the British Isles.
St. Columba, the Apostle of Caledonia, 521-597.
St. Augustin of Canterbury and the Roman Missionaries in England, 597-633.
The Celtic Monks and the Anglo-Saxons.
St. Wilfrid establishes Roman Unity and the Benedictine Order, 634-709.
Contemporaries and Successors of St. Wilfrid, 650-735.
Social and Political Influence of the Monks among the Anglo-Saxons.
The Anglo-Saxon Nuns.
The Church and the Feudal System—The Monastic Orders and Society.
St. Gregory, Monk and Pope.
The Predecessors of Calixtus II.

Times.

"Whatever the Count touches he of necessity adorns. He has produced a great and most interesting work, full of curious facts, and lit up with most noble eloquence."

Freeman's Journal.

"Of the translation, we must say it is in every respect worthy the original. The nervous style of the author is admirably preserved. It is at the same time spirited and faithful."

Standard.

"No library of English history will be complete without these glowing pictures of the 'Monks of the West.'"

NOTE.—Very few sets of this important and well-known work are now left for sale.

14 King William Street, Strand, London, W.C.

STANDARD HISTORICAL WORKS—continued.

The Lives of the Queens of Scotland,

AND ENGLISH PRINCESSES CONNECTED WITH THE REGAL SUCCESSION OF GREAT BRITAIN.

By AGNES STRICKLAND.

With Portraits and Historical Vignettes.

Eight Volumes, post 8vo, cloth, £4, 4s. *net*. Also in full calf and half calf bindings.

(*Published by* Messrs. W. BLACKWOOD & SONS, *Edinburgh*.)

CONTENTS OF THE WORK.

- Life of Margaret Tudor, Queen of James IV.
- Life of Magdalene of France, First Queen of James V.
- Life of Mary of Lorraine, Second Queen of James V.
- Life of the Lady Margaret Douglas, Countess of Lennox.
- Life of Mary Stuart, Queen of Scotland.
- Life of Elizabeth Stuart, First Princess Royal of Great Britain.
- Life of Sophia, Electress of Hanover.

English Review.

"Miss Strickland has not only been fortunate in the selection of her subject, but she has sustained to the full her high reputation for research."

The Standard.

"In 'The Queens of Scotland' Miss Strickland prosecutes her original task with as careful research as in her first work, and with undiminished spirit and unaltered delicacy."

The Guardian.

"We discern freedom and ease of manner, a judicious selection of materials, an evenly balanced judgment, and the sobriety and decision which are the fruits of wide historical knowledge."

Blackwood's Magazine.

"Every step in Scotland is historical; the shades of the dead arise on every side; the very rocks breathe. Miss Strickland's talents as a writer, and turn of mind as an individual, in a peculiar manner fit her for painting a historical gallery of the most illustrious or dignified female characters in that land of chivalry and song."

NOTE.—Very few sets of this delightful work are now left for sale.

14 King William Street, Strand, London, W.C.

OCTAVE UZANNE'S ILLUSTRATED WORKS.

Royal 8vo, cloth, gilt top, Illustrations engraved in colours, price 42s. *net.*

The Frenchwoman of the Century.
FASHIONS—MANNERS—USAGES.
By OCTAVE UZANNE.

Illustrations in Water Colours by ALBERT LYNCH. Engraved in Colours by EUGÈNE GAUJEAN.

Morning Post.—"Graceful and light as is this book by M. Octave Uzanne, the clever author of 'The Fan' and 'The Sunshade, Muff, and Glove,' and other works marked by a rare originality, it affords a more complete insight into the ideas of the women of France of this century and of the influence exercised by them than is apparent on the surface. An idea can be formed of the prodigality and luxury that prevailed at the Court of the First Empire by 'a serio-comic document' circulated in 1807 as 'an account of the annual expense of a female fop of Paris.' Its different items amount to the sum of 190,000fr., or £7600 sterling. The women of fashion of a later period are not less well photographed. There are some sparkling pages on those of 1830, at the time when Balzac discovered and sang 'La Femme de Trente Ans,' 'whose beauty shines with all the brightness of a perfumed summer.' Speaking the truth always, but with native gallantry seeking to conceal its harshness, M. Uzanne tells his countrywomen of to-day that 'the woman of this end of the century reigns despotically still in our hearts, but has no longer the same happy influence on our spirits, our manners, our society.' To account for this, as indeed in writing the moral aspect of all the different social phases that come within his scope, the author reasons of cause and effect with an able lucidity that skilfully avoids dulness. The illustrations are, without exception, artistic and *spirituelle*, and contribute to make of this elegantly bound work, a veritable 'volume de luxe,' which worthily continues the series of productions from M. Uzanne's brilliant and facile pen."

Royal 8vo, cloth, gilt top, 31s. 6d. *net.*

THE FAN. By OCTAVE UZANNE.
Illustrations by PAUL AVRIL.

Standard.—"It gives a complete history of fans of all ages and places; the illustrations are dainty in the extreme. Those who wish to make a pretty and appropriate present to a young lady cannot do better than purchase 'The Fan.'"

Athenæum.—"The letterpress comprises much amusing 'chit-chat,' and is more solid than it pretends to be. This *brochure* is worth reading; nay, it is worth keeping."

Royal 8vo, cloth, gilt top, 31s. 6d. *net.*

The Sunshade, Muff, and Glove.
By OCTAVE UZANNE.
Illustrations by PAUL AVRIL.

Art Journal.—"At first sight it would seem that material could never be found to fill even a volume; but the author, in dealing with his first subject alone, 'The Sunshade,' says he could easily have filled a dozen volumes of this emblem of sovereignty. The work is delightfully illustrated in a novel manner by Paul Avril, the pictures which meander about the work being printed in various colours."

---

14 King William Street, Strand, London, W.C.

Charming Editions, Illustrated with Etchings, of Standard Works, suitable for presentation. Crown 8vo, handsomely bound, either in cloth or parchment bindings, price 7s. 6d. per volume.

1. **THE TALES AND POEMS OF EDGAR ALLAN POE.** With Biographical Essay by JOHN H. INGRAM; and Fourteen Original Etchings, Three Photogravures, and a Portrait newly etched from a lifelike Daguerrotype of the Author. In Four Volumes.
2. **WEIRD TALES.** By E. T. W. HOFFMAN. A New Translation from the German. With Biographical Memoir by J. T. BEALBY, formerly Scholar of Corpus Christi College, Cambridge. With Portrait and Ten Original Etchings by AD. LALAUZE. In Two Volumes.
3. **THE LIFE AND OPINIONS OF TRISTRAM SHANDY,** GENTLEMAN. By LAURENCE STERNE. In Two Vols. With Eight Etchings by DAMMAN from Original Drawings by HARRY FURNISS.
4. **THE OLD ENGLISH BARON:** A GOTHIC STORY. By CLARA REEVE. **THE CASTLE OF OTRANTO:** A GOTHIC STORY. By HORACE WALPOLE. In One Vol. With Two Portraits and Four Original Drawings by A. H. TOURRIER, Etched by DAMMAN.
5. **THE ARABIAN NIGHTS ENTERTAINMENTS.** In Four Vols. Carefully Revised and Corrected from the Arabic by JONATHAN SCOTT, LL.D., Oxford. With Nineteen Original Etchings by AD. LALAUZE.
6. **THE HISTORY OF THE CALIPH VATHEK.** By WM. BECKFORD. With Notes, Critical, and Explanatory. **RASSELAS, PRINCE OF ABYSSINIA.** By SAMUEL JOHNSON. In One Vol. With Portrait of BECKFORD, and Four Original Etchings, designed by A. H. TOURRIER, and Etched by DAMMAN.
7. **ROBINSON CRUSOE.** By DANIEL DEFOE. In Two Vols. With Biographical Memoir, Illustrative Notes, and Eight Etchings by M. MOUILLERON, and Portrait by L. FLAMENG.
8. **GULLIVER'S TRAVELS.** By JONATHAN SWIFT. With Five Etchings and Portrait by AD. LALAUZE.
9. **A SENTIMENTAL JOURNEY.** By LAURENCE STERNE. **A TALE OF A TUB.** By JONATHAN SWIFT. In One Vol. With Five Etchings and Portrait by ED. HEDOUIN.
10. **THE HISTORY OF DON QUIXOTE DE LA MANCHA.** Translated from the Spanish of MIGUEL DE CERVANTES SAAVEDRA by MOTTEUX. With copious Notes (including the Spanish Ballads), and an Essay on the Life and Writings of CERVANTES by JOHN G. LOCKHART. Preceded by a Short Notice of the Life and Works of PETER ANTHONY MOTTEUX by HENRI VAN LAUN. Illustrated with Sixteen Original Etchings by R. DE LOS RIOS. Four Volumes.
11. **LAZARILLO DE TORMES.** By Don DIEGO MENDOZA. Translated by THOMAS ROSCOE. And **GUZMAN D'ALFARACHE.** By MATEO ALEMAN. Translated by BRADY. Illustrated with Eight Original Etchings by R. DE LOS RIOS. Two Volumes.
12. **ASMODEUS.** By LE SAGE. Translated from the French. Illustrated with Four Original Etchings by R. DE LOS RIOS.
13. **THE BACHELOR OF SALAMANCA.** By LE SAGE. Translated from the French by JAMES TOWNSEND. Illustrated with Four Original Etchings by R. DE LOS RIOS.

Continued next page.

14 King William Street, Strand, London, W.C.

Continued from page 18.

14. **VANILLO GONZALES**; or, The Merry Bachelor. By LE SAGE. Translated from the French. Illustrated with Four Original Etchings by R. DE LOS RIOS.

15. **THE ADVENTURES OF GIL BLAS OF SANTILLANE.** Translated from the French of LE SAGE by TOBIAS SMOLLETT. With Biographical and Critical Notice of LE SAGE by GEORGE SAINTSBURY. New Edition, carefully revised. Illustrated with Twelve Original Etchings by R. DE LOS RIOS. Three Volumes.

The Times.

"Among the numerous handsome reprints which the publishers of the day vie with each other in producing, we have seen nothing of greater merit than this series of volumes. Those who have read these masterpieces of the last century in the homely garb of the old editions may be gratified with the opportunity of perusing them with the advantages of large clear print and illustrations of a quality which is rarely bestowed on such reissues. The series deserves every commendation."

Royal 8vo, cloth extra, printed in colours and gilt top, price 12s. 6d.

An elegant and choicely Illustrated Edition of

GOLDSMITH'S VICAR OF WAKEFIELD.

With Prefatory Memoir by GEORGE SAINTSBURY,

And One Hundred and Fourteen Coloured Illustrations by V. A. POIRSON (Illustrator of "Gulliver's Travels").

Saturday Review.

"Goldsmith's immortal tale is here delightfully illustrated in colour, and there is a prefatory memoir by Mr. George Saintsbury, full of delicate criticism and careful research. The illustrations are sketchy, fresh, merry, and in colours perfectly harmonious. Such a book is a boon to the cultivated reader of every age."

The Guardian.

"A new edition of the 'Vicar of Wakefield' naturally appears with every fresh variety of the arts of printing or illustration. M. Poirson showed so keen an appreciation of the peculiar humour of 'Gulliver's Travels,' that it was only to be expected that he should try his hand at an even more popular book. Mr. Saintsbury has prefixed an excellent critical memoir, and altogether, if Goldsmith could have chosen the garb in which he would best like his Vicar to appear, his ideas would probably have jumped with those of the present publisher."

The Graphic.

"They are indeed some of the most excellent specimens of artistic colour-printing now to be seen; and the book is a wonder of cheapness, seeing it is sold at the low sum of 12s. 6d."

---

14 King William Street, Strand, London, W.C.

A New and Beautiful Edition of the Imitation of Christ.

In demy 8vo, with Fifteen Etchings, bound in full white parchment, gilt top, price 21s. *net.*

The Imitation of Christ.

FOUR BOOKS.

Translated from the Latin by Rev. W. BENHAM, B.D.,
Rector of St. Edmund, King and Martyr, Lombard Street, London.

The text and quaint borders printed in brown ink on fine vellum paper, and illustrated with Fifteen Etchings by L. FLAMENG and CH. WALTNER, from designs by J. P. LAURENS and HENRY LEVY, printed on Japanese paper, make this, for presentation purposes, one of the most beautiful editions at present to be had.

Scotsman.
"We have not seen a more beautiful edition of 'The Imitation of Christ' than this one for many a day."

Magazine of Art.
"This new edition of the 'Imitation' may fairly be regarded as a work of art. It is well and clearly printed; the paper is excellent; each page has its peculiar border, and it is illustrated with fifteen etchings. Further than that the translation is Mr. Benham's we need say nothing more."

Second Edition, post 8vo, cloth elegant, gilt top, price 5s.

Carols and Poems.

FROM THE FIFTEENTH CENTURY TO THE PRESENT TIME.

Edited by A. H. BULLEN, B.A.

NOTE.—120 copies printed on fine medium 8vo paper, with Seven Illustrations on Japanese paper. Each copy numbered.

Saturday Review.
"Since the publication of Mr. Sandys's collection there have been many books issued on carols, but the most complete by far that we have met with is Mr. Bullen's new volume, 'Carols and Poems from the Fifteenth Century to the Present Time.' The preface contains an interesting account of Christmas festivities and the use of carols. Mr. Bullen has exercised great care in verifying and correcting the collections of his predecessors, and he has joined to them two modern poems by Hawker, two by Mr. William Morris, and others by Mr. Swinburne, Mr. Symonds, and Miss Rossetti. Altogether this is one of the most welcome books of the season."

---

14 King William Street, Strand, London, W.C.

Two Very Funny and Humorously Illustrated Books by

A. B. FROST.

Crown 8vo, cloth, gilt top, with One Hundred Illustrations, price 5s.

RUDDER GRANGE. By FRANK R. STOCKTON.

The Times.—"Many of the smaller drawings are wonderfully spirited; there are sketchy suggestions of scenery, which recall the pregnant touches of Bewick; and the figures of animals and of human types are capital, from the row of roosting fowls at the beginning of the chapter to the dilapidated tramp standing hat in hand."

Court and Society Review.—"After looking at the pictures we found ourselves reading the book again, and enjoying Pomona and her reading, and her adventure with the lightning rodder, and her dog-fight as much as·ever. And to read it twice over is the greatest compliment you can pay to a book of American humour."

Art Journal.—"Mr. Stockton, the author, and Mr. Frost, the artist, have here gone hand in hand to produce the most humorous of stories with the best results."

Morning Post.—"It will be welcomed in its new dress by many who have already made the acquaintance of Euphemia and Pomona, as well as by many who will now meet those excellent types of feminine character for the first time."

Saturday Review.—"The new edition of 'Rudder Grange' has a hundred illustrations by Mr. A. B. Frost; they are extremely good, and worthy of Mr. Stockton's amusing book."

Small 4to, One Hundred and Twenty Illustrations, price 6s.

STUFF AND NONSENSE. By A. B. FROST.

CONTENTS.

The Fatal Mistake—A Tale of a Cat.	*The Mule and the Crackers.*
Ye Æsthete, ye Boy, and ye Bullfrog.	*The Influence of Kindness.*
The Balloonists.	*Bobby and the Little Green Apples.*
The Powers of the Human Eye.	*The Awful Comet.*
The Crab-Boy and His Elephant.	*The Tug of War.*
The Old Man of Moriches.	*The Ironical Flamingo.*
The Bald-headed Man.	&c. &c. &c.

Standard.—"This is a book which will please equally people of all ages. The illustrations are not only extremely funny, but they are drawn with wonderful artistic ability, and are full of life and action.

"It is far and away the best book of 'Stuff and Nonsense' which has appeared for a long time."

Press.—"The most facetious bit of wit that has been penned for many a day, both in design and text, is Mr. A. B. Frost's 'Stuff and Nonsense.' 'A Tale of a Cat' is funny, 'The Balloonists' is perhaps rather extravagant, but nothing can outdo the wit of 'The Powers of the Human Eye,' whilst 'Ye Æsthete, ye Boy, and ye Bullfrog' may be described as a 'roarer.' Mr. Frost's pen and pencil know how to chronicle fun, and their outcomes should not be overlooked."

Graphic.—"Grotesque in the extreme. His jokes will rouse many a laugh."

---

14 King William Street, Strand, London, W.C.

IMAGINARY CONVERSATIONS.
By WALTER SAVAGE LANDOR.

In Five Vols. crown 8vo, cloth, 30s.

FIRST SERIES—CLASSICAL DIALOGUES, GREEK AND ROMAN.
SECOND SERIES—DIALOGUES OF SOVEREIGNS AND STATESMEN.
THIRD SERIES—DIALOGUES OF LITERARY MEN.
FOURTH SERIES—DIALOGUES OF FAMOUS WOMEN.
FIFTH SERIES—MISCELLANEOUS DIALOGUES.

NOTE.—*This New Edition is printed from the last Edition of his Works, revised and edited by John Forster, and is published by arrangement with the Proprietors of the Copyright of Walter Savage Landor's Works.*

The Times.

"The abiding character of the interest excited by the writings of Walter Savage Landor, and the existence of a numerous band of votaries at the shrine of his refined genius, have been lately evidenced by the appearance of the most remarkable of Landor's productions, his 'Imaginary Conversations,' taken from the last edition of his works. To have them in a separate publication will be convenient to a great number of readers."

The Athenæum.

"The appearance of this tasteful reprint would seem to indicate that the present generation is at last waking up to the fact that it has neglected a great writer, and if so, it is well to begin with Landor's most adequate work. It is difficult to overpraise the 'Imaginary Conversations.' The eulogiums bestowed on the 'Conversations' by Emerson will, it is to be hoped, lead many to buy this book."

Scotsman.

"An excellent service has been done to the reading public by presenting to it, in five compact volumes, these 'Conversations.' Admirably printed on good paper, the volumes are handy in shape, and indeed the edition is all that could be desired. When this has been said, it will be understood what a boon has been conferred on the reading public; and it should enable many comparatively poor men to enrich their libraries with a work that will have an enduring interest."

BOOK-CORNER PROTECTORS.

Metal Tips carefully prepared for placing on the Corners of Books to preserve them from injury while passing through the Post Office or being sent by Carrier.

Extract from "The Times," April 18th.

"That the publishers and booksellers second the efforts of the Post Office authorities in endeavouring to convey books without damage happening to them is evident from the tips which they use to protect the corners from injury during transit."

1s. 6d. per Gross, *net*.

---

14 King William Street, Strand, London, W.C.

The American Patent Portable Book-Case.

For Students, Barristers, Home Libraries, &c.

This Book-case will be found to be made of very solid and durable material, and of a neat and elegant design. The shelves may be adjusted for books of any size, and will hold from 150 to 300 volumes. As it requires neither nails, screws, or glue, it may be taken to pieces in a few minutes, and reset up in another room or house, where it would be inconvenient to carry a large frame.

Full Height, 5 ft. 11½ in. ; *Width,* 3 ft. 8 inch ; *Depth of Shelf,* 10½ in.
Black Walnut, price £6, 6s. net.

"The accompanying sketch illustrates a handy portable book-case of American manufacture, which Mr. Nimmo has provided. It is quite different from an ordinary article of furniture, such as upholsterers inflict upon the public, as it is designed expressly for holding the largest possible number of books in the smallest possible amount of space. One of the chief advantages which these book-cases possess is the ease with which they may be taken apart and put together again. No nails or metal screws are employed, nothing but the hand is required to dismantle or reconstruct the case. The parts fit together with mathematical precision; and, from a package of boards of very moderate dimensions, a firm and substantial book-case can be erected in the space of a few minutes. Appearances have by no means been overlooked; the panelled sides, bevelled edges, and other simple ornaments, give to the cases a very neat and tasteful look. For students, or others whose occupation may involve frequent change of residence, these book-cases will be found most handy and desirable, while, at the same time, they are so substantial, well-made, and convenient, that they will be found equally suitable for the library at home."

14 King William Street, Strand, London, W.C.

www.ingramcontent.com/pod-product-compliance
Lightning Source LLC
Chambersburg PA
CBHW020824230426
43666CB00007B/1101